THE MANY ISLANDS
OF POLYNESIA

CONTENTS

LIST OF ILLUSTRATIONS

Prologue

The first European to see the Pacific by approaching from its west side may have been a Portuguese. Vasco da Gama had reached India in 1498 by sailing around Africa, and Portuguese explorers continued to push eastward in the dozen years that followed, conquering the port of Malacca on the strait northwest of Singapore in 1511. From there an expedition under the command of Francisco Serrão soon explored still farther east. In 1512 Serrão settled at the island of Ternate in the northern Moluccas; it is considered probable that on a voyage from there he became the first European to see the open Pacific.

On September 25, 1513, Vasco Núñez de Balboa, a Spaniard, first saw the Pacific from the east, from a mountaintop on the Isthmus of Panama. After struggling through the jungle to the beach, he waded into the new ocean, claiming it and all lands and islands touching it in the name of the King of Spain. A glance at the map shows that the Isthmus of Panama runs east and west, so this body of water lay to the south and was christened the Great South Sea by its discoverer.

Somewhere beyond this ocean lay Asia and the Moluccas, the rich Spice Islands. How to get a ship into it was the question. Even as early as this a canal through Panama was suggested. But perhaps some natural waterway led through America, or perhaps one could sail northwest around North America or southwest around South America.

Ferdinand Magellan, a Portuguese-born navigator who had taken Spanish citizenship, found a route. With five ships, ranging in size from 75 to 120 tons (the deck length of the largest might have been 80 feet), he sailed from Spain on September 20, 1519, seeking a way to the Great South Sea. He searched the coast of South America for over eight months, but found no passage through the continent. Food grew short and the men became discontent as cold weather approached. After wintering on the coast of what is now Argentina, Magellan continued south and came upon a waterway which was later named the Strait of Magellan. It took Magellan thirty-eight days to get his ships through this treacherous passage to the South Sea. He had only three vessels left; one had been wrecked, and the captain of his largest ship had deserted and headed for Spain with much of the fleet's provisions.

Magellan entered the big ocean on November 28, 1520, sailed north along the coast for some days, then headed northwest before the trade winds. The water seemed so calm after the storms of the Strait that he renamed the ocean the Pacific. For three months he sailed across the Pacific, sighting only two uninhabited islands and finding no food or fresh water. The little water left in the casks was loathsomely stagnant; rats became prized for food, and even sawdust was eaten. Many of the sailors died of scurvy and other diseases.

Finally, after ninety-eight days in the Pacific, the weary seafarers sighted the island of Guam. They stayed only a few days, obtaining fresh fruit, meat, and water, which rapidly began to restore the survivors. Magellan (as did many later European visitors) found that the natives looked upon property ownership very casually, tending to take anything they fancied. After one of his small boats and various other items were stolen, Magellan named the islands Ladrones, or Islands of Thieves. Today the group bears a pleasanter name, the Mariana Islands.

After sailing westward for another week, Magellan came to the Philippines, where he stopped at several islands and succeeded in converting the rajah of Cebu to Christianity. Unfortunately, Magellan decided to help his new convert with a military expedition against a rival island, and he was killed on April 27, 1521, along with a number of his men. One of the Spanish vessels, the *Victoria*, was the first ship to circumnavigate the earth, finally arriving back in Spain on September 6, 1522. The first person to circumnavigate the earth was Enrique, Magellan's slave. He had come to Spain from somewhere in the Moluccas or the Philippines and so completed his around-the-world voyage when the Spaniards still had nearly half the distance to go.

In the decade after the return of the *Victoria*, more Spanish expeditions were sent out from Spain and, later, from new Pacific outposts in Mexico and South America. Additional islands were discovered in what are now the Marshall and Caroline groups, and New Guinea was sighted. All of the early Pacific crossings were in a westerly (east to west) direction; several attempts to return failed when the ships ran into strong head winds.

In 1564 five ships under Miguel López de Legazpi sailed from Mexico to the Philippines to colonize new islands and to find a way back across the Pacific. Two skillful pilots in the expedition succeeded in finding a west-to-east return route by heading north in a great circle that went as far as 40° above the equator. Favorable winds and currents along this course took the ships to the California coast.

This route was the standard one followed by the Spanish galleons from 1565 to 1815. The trip west from Acapulco to Manila, in the northeast trade winds above the equator, took about three months, including a short stop at Guam for provisions and water. The return voyage took five or six months. Two galleons per year sailed in each direction. Westward they carried Mexican silver, copper, and other commodities; eastward they carried silks, ivory, china, spices, and jewelry. Much of this cargo was carried across Mexico, then shipped across the Atlantic to Spain.

One may wonder why the galleons, in about a thousand crossings of the Pacific, did not discover the Hawaiian Islands. In fact, their standard routes (which as government-controlled passenger and cargo vessels they had to follow) were too far to the

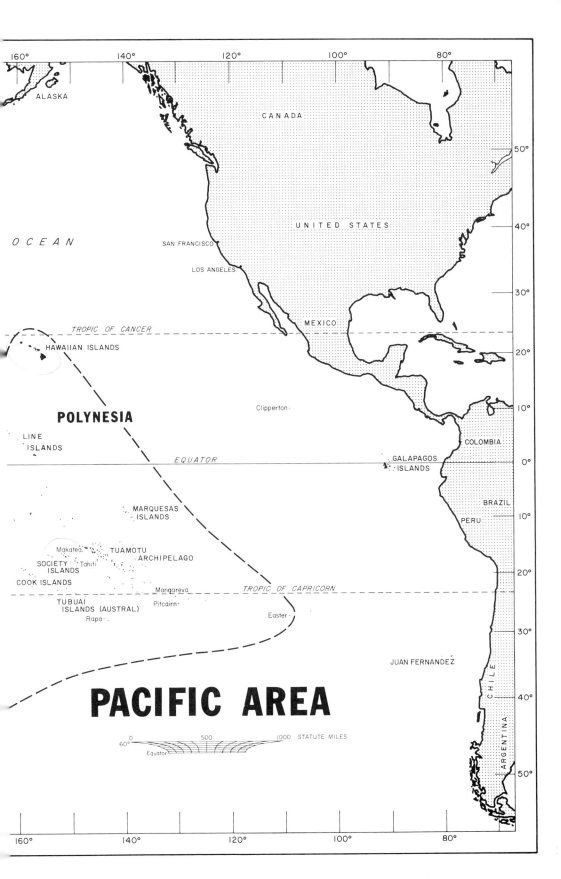

south on the westward voyages and much too far to the north as they returned east for any but accidental sightings. If any Spanish ships did stray off course and become wrecked in Hawaii, no survivors ever returned to report the existence of these large and fruitful islands which would have made a fine mid-ocean stop. Hawaii awaited Captain Cook.

Three Spanish expeditions from South America into the Pacific deserve special mention. In 1567 two ships under Alvaro de Mendaña sailed from Peru. Although they sighted a few reefs and islets, they did not land until they had crossed the Pacific and arrived at a group of large mountainous islands in what is now called Melanesia. Although the inhabitants soon proved to be hostile—headhunters and cannibals—Mendaña thought that gold and silver might be found there, and his expedition remained in these waters for six months before sailing north and then east to California. Although no treasure was brought back, the lure of these islands and their riches grew in tales told by adventurers until it was felt certain that they were the site of the legendary mines of King Solomon. And so they became known —as they still are—as the Solomon Islands. But they were not rediscovered for two centuries.

Mendaña took more than twenty-five years to gather enough financial support for a second expedition, which sailed in June of 1595. He could not find the Solomons again, but he did discover the Marquesas, the first important group of Polynesian islands, only five weeks after leaving Peru. Although he noted the handsomeness of the Marquesan men and the grace of their women, several hundred of them were killed, some apparently just for target practice, by the firearms of the Spaniards during their two-week stay. Continuing westward, Mendaña passed only a few low-lying atolls before he discovered a group of volcanic islands, the Santa Cruz Islands, which lie east of the Solomons. Mendaña proceeded to establish a settlement there although he did not find the natives friendly; the general policy of the Spanish was to insist on friendship by force of arms.

Many of the men contracted fatal fevers, and Mendaña himself died about six weeks after discovering the Santa Cruz group.

The expedition's command passed to Mendaña's widow, Doña Isabel, a haughty, ruthless, self-centered woman whose fortune had helped finance the voyage. Through the skill of the pilot-major, Pedro Fernández de Quirós, the survivors of the expedition made their way to the Philippines while Doña Isabel ate well and the seamen starved. In the Philippines, Doña Isabel acquired a new Spanish husband and sailed back to America with him in a ship piloted by Quirós.

Quirós himself led three ships on a new search for the Solomon Islands in 1605. It had long been thought that a huge continent must exist somewhere in the Southern Hemisphere to counterbalance the large northern continents of Asia and Europe. This continent presumably contained vast resources of precious metals and jewels, as well as millions of heathens awaiting conversion to Christianity. The land to the south of the Strait of Magellan might be part of this continent, or perhaps many of the earlier explorers' land sightings were actually northern tips of this great undiscovered land called *Terra Australis Incognita* (the Unknown Southern Continent). Quirós felt that it lay not far from either the Solomon or the Santa Cruz islands.

On his way across the Pacific, Quirós discovered a number of small atolls, mostly in the Tuamotu Archipelago. He was unable to find either the Solomon or the Santa Cruz islands, but he did find a new group of high islands now called the New Hebrides. He named the principal island Austrialia del Espíritu Santo (in honor of Philip of Austria, not because he thought it was the sought-for *Australis*). This island is still called Espíritu Santo (Holy Spirit). After only a little more than two months there, however, Quirós, plagued by sickness and native hostility, sailed for Acapulco. His lieutenant, Luis Vaez de Torres, in one of the other ships, succeeded in reaching Manila by sailing to the south of New Guinea, thereby discovering the strait which still bears his name.

For most of the rest of Spain's period of dominance in the Pacific, her exploration concentrated on the American coasts, the Philippines, and parts of Micronesia.

Even as the sixteenth century was one of Spanish discovery in the Pacific, the first half of the seventeenth century was a time of Dutch exploration there. Having established their independence and naval power, the Dutch first approached the Pacific around the Cape of Good Hope, moved into the East Indies, and began to replace the Portuguese and Spanish in that area.

Most ships of the Dutch East India Company used the route around the Cape of Good Hope, but a few fleets dared the stormier passage through the Strait of Magellan. The East India Company, a large organization with commercial, political, and military powers, had received exclusive commercial rights to both these approaches from the Dutch government. But in 1616, Isaac Le Maire and Willem Schouten, a pair of independent Dutchmen, found a new route—south around the very tip of the Americas, which Le Maire called Cape Hoorn in honor of his home town. The Le Maire expedition also visited several islands in the Tuamotu Archipelago as well as some of the northern Tongan islands and the other small Polynesian islands of Futuna and Alofi, which they patriotically called the Hoorn Islands, before proceeding north of New Guinea to the Indies.

By the middle of the seventeenth century the Dutch skippers sailing around Africa to the East Indies had learned a good bit about the north, west, and south coasts of Australia, which they had named New Holland. (Some had learned the hard way—by running into it at night!) Still they did not know whether it was one mass of land or two, whether or not it was connected with New Guinea (the Spanish had kept the existence of Torres Strait a secret), or how far to the south or east it might extend. Its relation to the supposed *Terra Australis Incognita* was likewise obscure.

In August, 1642, Anthony van Diemen, governor-general of the East Indies, sent a two-ship expedition under Abel Janszoon Tasman to attempt to discover the great south continent, to rediscover the Solomon Islands, and to look for valuable minerals. Tasman's ten-month voyage followed a huge elliptical course which took him completely around both Australia and New Guinea. Indeed, he didn't sight Australia at all, for that was not his purpose. Nor did he locate the supposed south continent or the almost equally elusive Solomons. However, he did discover the large island of Van Diemen's Land (now called Tasmania) and New Zealand, where after a brief battle with the natives he decided it would be unsafe to land. Further north he discovered several groups of the Tongan islands and parts of Fiji. Probably the greatest of Dutch navigators, Tasman is also recognized on the map today by the name of the sea between Australia and New Zealand.

The last Dutch explorer of note, Jacob Roggeveen, left Holland for the Pacific by way of Cape Horn in August, 1721. On Easter Day, 1722, he discovered an inhabited island which he named Easter Island. Before arriving at the Indies, Roggeveen discovered some new islands in the widespread Tuamotu Archipelago and several of the eastern Samoan islands.

British privateers and buccaneers (little more than legalized pirates) had visited the Pacific since the time of Queen Elizabeth, more for the purpose of plundering Spanish settlements and capturing Spanish galleons than for exploration. Sir Francis Drake entered the Pacific in 1578, seizing a great deal of booty and visiting the coast of California before eluding Spanish warships by sailing all the way around the world. Before the end of the century, several more British expeditions attempted similar forays, of which that of Thomas Cavendish in 1587 was most successful. William Dampier, a very remarkable naval officer, was involved in some five Pacific expeditions between 1670 and 1711.

British activity in the Pacific increased during the middle of the eighteenth century. An expedition led by George Anson in the 1740's captured an extremely rich galleon. Expeditions primarily for exploration began in 1764, when John Byron sailed for the Pacific in the copper-sheathed *Dolphin*. Although he discovered little new, the same ship was sent out again in 1766 under Samuel Wallis, who became the first European to sight and land on Tahiti. His accompanying ship, the *Swallow*, under Philip Carteret, became separated from the *Dolphin* in a storm. It was successful in finding only uninhabited Pitcairn Island and a few other small islands on its crossing of the Pacific. Carteret also rediscovered one of the Solomon Islands, "lost" for two centuries, but did not identify it correctly.

Coincidentally, the French had sent forth an expedition under Louis Antoine de Bougainville. Bougainville came upon Tahiti only nine and a half months after Wallis' discovery, nearly a year before word of the island's existence reached Europe. In the western Pacific, Bougainville also sighted but did not identify the Solomon Islands.

The most distinguished, scientific, and brilliant sea explorer of all time was James Cook, an Englishman, who in three voyages into the Pacific discovered many yet unknown islands and obtained great amounts of other information about the Pacific. Considerate of his men and attentive to their welfare, meticulous in his observations and map making, and unusually skilled in his dealings with natives, he left his followers, as another explorer remarked, "little to do but admire his accomplishments." Captain Cook's first voyage (1768–1771) had as one major purpose the observation from a site on Tahiti of a rare astronomical event, the transit of Venus across the sun. A second purpose was to continue the work of South Pacific exploration, including further search for the still-believed-in *Terra Australis Incognita.*

After a stay of over three months at Tahiti, Cook sailed westward through neighboring islands, which he named the Society Islands, headed south, then cruised west once again until New Zealand was sighted. Cook spent six months exploring and mapping the New Zealand coastline, circumnavigating the North and South Islands and discovering the strait between them. In the process he demolished the possibility that New Zealand was a portion of *Terra Australis.* Cook next sailed across the Tasman Sea to Australia, discovering and mapping its hitherto unknown east coast, then proceeded north to rediscover and pass through Torres Strait. On this portion of his voyage, an encounter with the Great Barrier Reef nearly tore the bottom out of the *En-*

deavour. Only exceptional skill and coolness combined with good fortune enabled Cook to save his ship and repair her.

Nine months after returning to England, Cook set forth on another three-year expedition (1772–1775) intending to settle the matter of *Terra Australis* conclusively. This time provided with two ships, the *Resolution* and the *Adventure,* he sailed completely around the bottom of the world, going as far south as he dared on several occasions. He finally concluded that if any great southern continent existed, it must lie in polar waters. On this trip he also took several circular detours through the warmer parts of the South Pacific, calling twice at New Zealand and Tahiti, visiting Easter Island, the Marquesas, and Tonga, and discovering a number of new islands, including New Caledonia and Norfolk.

Having filled in many blanks on the map of the South Pacific, Cook set forth in 1776 in command of the *Resolution* and the *Discovery* to find out about the North Pacific: its outlines and the possibility of a northern passage leading to the Atlantic. Proceeding by way of the Cape of Good Hope, he called at Tasmania, New Zealand, Tonga, and Tahiti. Although a few small islands were also discovered, the most important discovery by Cook's third expedition was the Hawaiian Islands, or the Sandwich Islands, as he called them, which he first sighted on January 18, 1778. After a two-week stay in these waters, Cook proceeded to North America, mapping various portions of the coast and continuing through the Bering Strait until he was forced back by ice.

With winter coming, Cook headed back to the warm Hawaiian waters, where he found that he had missed the two biggest islands of the group on his trip north. He sighted Maui on November 26, 1778, and went on to the big island of Hawaii, where on February 14, 1779, the great explorer, perhaps the most skillful of all early Pacific visitors in dealing with the natives, ironically met his death in a brief, unexpected battle with the Hawaiians. The expedition spent one more summer exploring the North Pacific before heading back to England. Other Englishmen, including William Bligh, George Bass, Matthew

Flinders, and George Vancouver, made further important con-
tributions to the knowledge of the Pacific and the waters around
Australia, but Captain Cook remains the giant of Pacific exploration.

The nineteenth century brought additional British and
French voyagers and some Russians as well into the Pacific.
Russia had established North Pacific outposts in Siberia and
Alaska before 1800 and in the next twenty-five years sent out
about ten expeditions which visited the South Pacific.

The United States was in its early years an Atlantic nation,
looking back across the ocean toward Europe. The history of
America since has included, among other changes, a shift away
from its being an exclusively Atlantic nation toward being an
Atlantic *and* Pacific nation.

An interest in the Pacific was shown in the early years of the
United States among seafarers, especially the Yankee captains
from Salem and Boston in the China trade and, later, those who
sailed from such ports as Nantucket, New Bedford, Mystic, and
New London in quest of whales. The China trade, which started
before 1800, was at its height a three-stage enterprise: the ships
would leave the east coast of the United States loaded with
relatively cheap goods attractive to the Pacific islanders or to the
Pacific Coast Indians and trade the goods to them for items
which were in demand in China—sea-otter skins from the Northwest and sandalwood from the larger Pacific islands. From the
Chinese, in turn, the traders obtained goods which would sell
at a profit back home—tea, silks, porcelains, and chinaware. Fur
seals, found on the Falkland and other islands near the tip of
South America, were also hunted and their skins taken across
the Pacific to China. Other important items in the China trade
included pearls and mother-of-pearl shells, tortoise shell, and
bêche-de-mer. *

Many of the ships in the China trade went completely around

*Also called trepang; a marine animal also known as the sea cucumber. It can be
preserved by drying and is used in certain Chinese soups.

the world on their voyages, entering the Pacific by Cape Horn and returning around the Cape of Good Hope, although the reverse direction was sometimes used. The first American ship to sail around the world, the *Columbia,* on its second voyage in the fur trade, sailed into the large river on the west coast which still bears the ship's name.

But during the first half of the nineteenth century, whalers were the most numerous American ships in the Pacific. Particularly when the War of 1812 made the Atlantic unsafe for American whalers, they turned to the Pacific. In the decades that followed, although one by one certain areas were depleted of whales, new grounds were continually being discovered in the vast ocean. Whale oil was in great demand as a fuel for lanterns and as a lubricant; from the sperm whale came an oil of exceptionally fine quality as well as a waxy substance used to make the finest candles. Whalebone, used in ladies' corsets and other articles, also had a good market.

The industry boomed. In 1840 five hundred American whalers were cruising in the Pacific. The supply of whales seemed inexhaustible, but it wasn't. In the 1850's and thereafter, as whales grew scarce, expeditions more expensive, and other sources of oil—especially petroleum—came into use, the whaling industry rapidly declined.

American commercial and whaling ships obtained much general information about the Pacific; scientific knowledge was gathered by the United States Exploring Expedition (1838–1842) under Lieutenant Charles Wilkes, whose extensive reports were published in five volumes and many additional papers. Another large American expedition (1853–1856) explored North Pacific waters.

America's territorial interest in the Pacific islands came through a rapid series of events at the turn of the century. True, the United States had been given the rights to establish a naval coaling station at Samoa in 1872 and had likewise obtained the rights to use Pearl Harbor by an 1887 treaty, though no work had been done on its development. But in 1898 the Spanish-American War brought the Pacific, its islands, and the United

States Navy into new prominence. When this short war was over, the United States had acquired Guam and the Philippines. In the same year the Republic of Hawaii was annexed by the United States. The eastern part of Samoa came under American ownership in 1899 through a treaty with Britain and Germany, and in 1900 Hawaii was finally organized as an American Territory.

Twentieth-century developments have continued to increase America's concern with the Pacific and Asia. The Panama Canal, opened in 1914, made the Pacific more readily accessible to both merchant and naval vessels from the Atlantic. World War II brought the United States into armed conflict with Japan, then the most powerful military force in Asia, and left the United States as temporary administrator of a number of islands that had been Japanese possessions. Most of Micronesia came under American administration as a Trust Territory of the United Nations. The Philippines were granted their independence in 1946, and Hawaii became the fiftieth of the United States in 1959, but American military involvements in Korea and Vietnam are two more indications that the United States has not turned her back on the western Pacific.

Commerce in the Pacific has continued to grow. The great ocean is kept active with commercial shipping. Freighters, passenger ships, and tankers cross the Pacific en route to Hong Kong, Taiwan, Australia, New Zealand, Indonesia, the Philippines, Malaysia, Burma, Thailand, Vietnam, Korea, and dozens of islands. Japan, opened to commerce in 1854 but devastated during World War II, is again one of the world's great industrial nations, and about thirty percent of her exports go to this country. Trade with China may again become important. In all, the Pacific trade of the United States is increasing faster than that with any other region of the world.

The American tourist and the American travel industry have also become vitally interested in the Pacific. Many Pacific areas are placing in tourism their greatest hope for economic growth. New United States air routes into the area, granted in 1969, make Pacific travel more convenient and varied. In recommending these new routes, Robert Park, the Civil Aeronautics Board examiner, stated the point developed in the last few pages: "From every point of view—defense, the economy, trade, tourism—the interests of the United States are being drawn inexorably toward the countries of the Pacific Basin."

But let us look back at the Pacific as the early European visitors found it—a vast ocean containing thousands of islands, almost all of the larger ones inhabited by previously unknown races of dark-skinned peoples speaking strange languages and adhering to strange religions. They were self-sufficient, making their own clothing, canoes, and shelter from indigenous materials; they were skilled in agriculture, seafaring, and fishing; yet they possessed only a few domestic animals and lacked metals and systems of writing. What was the effect on them of the invasion by Europeans with their huge ships, their woven clothing, and their firearms?

In general the foreign incursion caused many drastic, often fatal, changes over a comparatively short period of time. The fascinating history of the Pacific, a region which has attained the

A modern freighter sails out the Golden Gate into the Pacific.

legendary status of an earthly paradise, has many sad chapters. The peoples, in many instances, lost their customs, their religion, their mode of government, their self-sufficiency, their identity, and sometimes their land. They fell prey to foreign diseases— tuberculosis, smallpox, measles, leprosy, venereal diseases—to which they had never been exposed and to which they had no immunity. These changes took place at different rates, in different degrees, and with different effects in various parts of the Pacific. Yet the Pacific made an unbreakable link with western civilization, and Pacific islanders are still faced with many problems related to the process that started with Magellan.

The Pacific Ocean is certainly the biggest single geographical feature our earth possesses. But one must distinguish between the Pacific Basin of today, the Pacific Ocean, and the True Pacific Basin of the past. Today's Pacific Basin runs 9,200 miles from the narrow Bering Strait between Asia and North America south to Antarctica and from the Americas west to Indonesia, a distance which in one line is over 12,000 miles, nearly half the distance around the globe. The Pacific Ocean proper fills most of the area, but at its western edge are a number of seas, or branches, separated from the ocean by groups of islands: the two China Seas, the Coral Sea, the Tasman Sea, and others. The total water area in the ocean and its adjacent seas is more than that of all the other oceans and seas in the world and more than the world's entire land area. Many scientists believe that perhaps once our earth had only one huge ocean and one land mass, and that the Pacific Ocean is the biggest part remaining of that one ocean after the land mass separated into continents and drifted over the earth's surface.

Scientists also speak of the "real" or "true" Pacific Basin, a region smaller than today's Pacific Ocean, which represents what the Pacific may have looked like a hundred million years ago, when the Australasian Continent extended farther to the south and east than it does today. The line marking the separation of the old continent from the rest of today's Pacific Ocean can easily be drawn on a map if you start from New Zealand and draw a line northerly which passes east of Tonga, Fiji, the Solomons, Yap, the Marianas, and Japan. This line is called the Andesite Line. The islands to the west are all, presumably, remains of the larger continent and are actually different in chemical composition from those which later rose from the bottom of the vast ocean to the east. Similarities and differences in plant and animal life on various Pacific islands are in part explained by the links and separations between some of these islands in the past.

The part of the Pacific Ocean lying within the "true"Basin is the deepest on earth, with an average depth of three miles. Several exceptionally deep areas, or trenches, just to the east of the Andesite Line, are from six to nearly seven miles deep.

Volcanic activity, past and present, and earthquakes are characteristic of Pacific regions all along the western coast of the Americas including the Aleutian Islands, in the islands to the west of the Andesite Line, and in many mid-ocean areas as well. The term "Ring of Fire" has been applied to the Pacific's volcanic encirclement.

Earthquakes in or near the Pacific, in addition to causing destruction directly on land, may cause *tsunami*s, or tidal waves, huge displacements of the ocean which can travel across the ocean at speeds up to five hundred miles per hour. These big movements across the ocean do not look like waves. In fact, if you were far at sea in a ship, you might not even notice one. But when a *tsunami* reaches land it rapidly creates a tremendously high tide which keeps rising and rising—ten, twenty, thirty or more feet above the normal water level, depending on the strength of the *tsunami* and the underwater characteristics of the area near the land—sweeping away trees, houses and other property, and sometimes causing great loss of life. Usually several big rises and falls of the water occur before a tidal wave finally ceases. On April 1, 1946, Hawaii was struck by its most disastrous tidal wave of the century, resulting in the loss of over one hundred and fifty lives and the destruction of twenty-five million dollars in property. While tidal waves cannot be prevented, seismology and radio communications today provide warning throughout the Pacific whenever a severe earthquake may have created one.

The number of islands in the Pacific can be counted as ten thousand, twenty-five thousand, thirty thousand, or just about any number in between. It all depends on how much ocean you choose to call the Pacific and what you wish to call an island. Is every piece of rock which sticks its head above water at low tide (or should it be high tide?) an island? By one estimate there are seven thousand islands in the Philippines alone! Likewise, there are a number of ways of classifying these islands—by area, by island groups or archipelagoes, and by types. One classification calls most of the larger islands west of the Andesite Line "continental islands" (since they are presumably remains of the old continent), and those to the east "oceanic islands." Then there are "high islands" and "low islands." The high islands, which include the continental islands and the oceanic islands of Hawaii, Samoa, Tahiti, and the Marquesas, range up to altitudes of three miles above sea level in New Guinea. High oceanic islands show evidence of the volcanic activity which brought them above the surface of the ocean; most high continental islands show the effects of volcanism upon their earlier continental makeup.

The low, or coral, islands are of two types: the atolls, of which good examples are found in the Tuamotu Archipelago, the Marshall and Gilbert Islands, and the raised coral islands, such as Nauru, Ocean, and Peleliu. The former are usually no more than a dozen feet above sea level; the latter may rise to over two hundred feet. Just to complicate matters, some islands, such as Guam, which is volcanic at one end and raised coral at the other, combine features of both high and low islands.

The formation of oceanic high islands is easy to understand, though rather amazing. From the bottom of the ocean, from depths of two or three miles, in a region where the earth's crust was weak, magma (liquid rock) poured forth, building a pile which, probably after many eruptions and a long time, finally extended to the surface of the ocean and above. The total elevation of such a mountain from base to top can be greater than that of the highest of the Himalayas, which start from an elevated

A portion of an atoll is a striking sight from the air.

plateau. Indeed, were the earth drained of all its water, the
biggest single bump on its surface would not be Mount Everest
but the island of Hawaii, which rises in one mass from over three
miles below sea level to nearly three miles above. Even a small
high island of the Pacific may be over a hundred miles in diameter at its sea-floor base.

But how about the low islands, whose structures are largely
made up of the skeletons and shells of small marine animals
called coral? In a living coral formation, only a very thin top
layer of coral is actually alive; below it lie the remains of myriads

of earlier generations. Study has shown that these creatures thrive only in warm seawater and only in depths up to perhaps two hundred feet. Yet some coral islands exist thousands of miles from any continent and rise from ocean floors many thousands of feet deep. How were they formed?

This problem faced the great Charles Darwin when he visited many coral islands of the Pacific aboard the *Beagle* in the early 1830's. His theory, which is still generally accepted, is that coral islands were originally mid-ocean islands, probably volcanic, along whose shores various forms of coral grew in shallow water. As the islands slowly sank from their own weight, or as the ocean rose (and the earth's oceans have had a number of large-scale rises and falls), the process was so slow that these creatures were able to continue to grow in a comfortable depth of water. The original island ended up far beneath the waves and beneath many feet of coral.

An "ideal" atoll, the result of a circular mountain slowly sinking beneath the waves in an area without strong ocean currents, might be doughnut-shaped, perhaps with some passes leading from the ocean into an inner lagoon. A number of atolls come quite close to this description; from the air they look like gigantic smoke rings of land. But more often the land mass which sank was irregular, or the atoll was worked upon by ocean forces which destroyed its symmetry. Kwajalein, the largest of the Marshall Islands, is the largest atoll in the world and, with a lagoon area of about eight hundred and forty square miles, is shaped like an imperfect boomerang with many large gaps in its perimeter.

Fringing reefs and barrier reefs are also coral structures. Fringing reefs, which occur in the shallow waters close to many of the Pacific islands, such as Hawaii, Fiji, and Tahiti, hug the shore and one can walk to or wade out on them from shore at low tide. A barrier reef is located some distance (often miles) from the shoreline and is generally parallel to it, with a lagoon or channel between it and the main body of land. Of these, the largest in the Pacific are those to the northeast of Australia (Great Barrier Reef) and New Caledonia. Since these formations also must have started to grow in shallow water, the barrier reef was once probably a fringing reef. As the island or continent sank or was eroded away, the busy coral polyps and algae kept growing, and today the reef remains.

By drilling holes into coral reefs and atolls, scientists have tried to determine how thick the coral is above the underlying rock. Early drillings in the Great Barrier Reef in 1928 and 1938 went down six or seven hundred feet and still brought up coral. Before using Bikini Atoll in the Marshall Islands for atomic experiments, American investigators drilled down over 2,500 feet and still found limy coral materials. Finally, seismic sounding, a method used elsewhere in seeking oil deposits, indicated that the actual solid rock of this atoll lies beneath seven thousand feet of coral. This finding revealed the tremendous amount of sinking that has taken place in the Pacific Basin as well as the great age of these structures. It may take two hundred years or more for coral to grow upward a single foot, and the process is slowed down, stopped, or even reversed by wave action during periods when prolonged lowering of the sea level exposes the coral to air.

Two other features of the Pacific can also be roughly outlined on a map: its major currents and winds. These characteristics are not as important to transportation today as they were in the days of wind-powered shipping, but they do have profound effects on Pacific weather. In general, on either side of the equator the surface currents move westerly. In the western Pacific they then move northward in a clockwise direction past Japan and the Aleutians, then south past the coast of North America. In the Southern Hemisphere the currents have a corresponding counterclockwise movement. Some of these major currents have branches, and land masses and seasonal changes affect their patterns. Currents at greater depths may run in entirely different directions.

Near the equator, in a region known as the doldrums, the winds are usually low and unpredictable. To the north and south of the doldrums, extending to about 30° latitude, lie the areas of the trade winds—northeast trades in the Northern Hemisphere and southeast trades in the Southern. The word "trade" here means "customary path or track," and it is applied because these winds blow about seventy percent of the time. Farther away from the equator, on both sides, lie regions in which the winds are customarily from the west; they are called the middle-latitude westerlies. In the far western Pacific the winds, called monsoons, are affected by the heating and cooling of the land mass of Asia, and they reverse their direction seasonally, causing regular rainy and dry seasons.

On both sides of the equator in the central and western Pacific, violent tropical storms known as typhoons or hurricanes often form. Hawaii used to be thought free of hurricanes—it merely had occasional bad storms. I learned that this idea was false in 1950 when a big wind, officially identified as Hawaii's first hurricane, turned my half-built house upside down.

Finally, extremely fast air currents called jet streams moving at several hundred miles per hour are sometimes encountered by airplanes at high altitudes above the Pacific.

Obviously there is a close relationship between people and their environment. Over thousands of years the peoples of the Pacific evolved a number of ways of life depending on the kind of island they lived on—its size, its rainfall, its temperature, its terrain, its soil, the presence or absence of a lagoon, the kinds of animal and vegetable life it would support. The coming of an alien civilization to the Pacific has, in one way or another, changed the old way of life, often removing both the need for and the knowledge of the old ways. And the Pacific islands are still changing rapidly. Yet even a century or two from now, they will doubtless still show a diversity which, fortunately, outside influences will not have entirely eliminated.

The Bishop Museum:
Storehouse of the Pacific

The best place in the world to go for information about the peoples, arts, sciences, and history of the Pacific islands is the Bernice Pauahi Bishop Museum in Honolulu. Princess Bernice Pauahi was the last in the Hawaiian royal line of Kamehamehas, but she declined to take the throne when Kamehameha V died in 1872. Married to a Honolulu businessman, Charles R. Bishop, she died childless in 1884, leaving her vast inheritance of royal lands as an estate to establish and support schools for children of Hawaiian descent. A few years after his wife's death, Mr. Bishop founded the Bernice Pauahi Bishop Museum in her memory for the purpose of engaging in research and providing publication and exhibition of materials dealing with the peoples and natural history of the Pacific. Dr. Roland W. Force, an anthropologist, has been the Museum's energetic director since 1962.

"Today we say that our task is scientific research in the natural and cultural history of the Pacific world," said Dr. Force. "In natural history we have departments of botany, entomology, and zoology, as well as a large geological collection. In cultural history, we have departments of anthropology and history. Our anthropologists—cultural anthropologists, ethnologists, archeologists, and ethnobotanists—are conducting work in all Pacific culture areas, with big projects in Hawaii and elsewhere."

Dr. Force then talked about the Museum's exhibits. To the left of the main entrance is a room for special exhibits, often artifacts of religious significance.

The Museum's pride is Hawaiian Hall, subtitled "The Heritage of the Fiftieth State," a three-story gallery with an open center space rising through its upper levels. The gallery is dominated by a huge, suspended whale's skeleton. One side has been reconstructed to show the appearance of the whale's body.

The bottom floor contains exhibits of ancient Hawaiian culture from before the arrival of Europeans. In the center are a model of a Hawaiian temple, or *heiau*, and a grass house. The large cases around the walls include displays of wooden and stone objects as well as Hawaiian cloth, *kapa* (or *tapa*)—beaten from bark and imprinted with dyes by the use of a pattern-bearing stick. *Tapa* is, or was, made on many other Pacific islands, but nowhere else was the cloth so soft or were the patterns so refined.

Of all the Hawaiian arts, the truly outstanding achievement was in featherwork, and some of the cases display beautiful feather leis, feather helmets, feather capes, feather cloaks, a feather skirt, and a fierce-looking feather-covered image—Kukailimoku, war god of Kamehameha.

The second level of Hawaiian Hall, "Conflict and Consonance: Monarchs, Mariners, Missionaries, Merchants," deals with Hawaiian acculturation—how the Hawaiians interacted with newcomers and the newcomers with one another. As Dr. Force says, "They either knocked heads and it didn't work, or they blended." Whaling is also the subject of several interesting exhibits on this level.

The third level, "Living in Harmony," shows Hawaii's later cultural heritage, from Europe, the Pacific, and Asia—from Portugal, Samoa, China, Japan, the Philippines, and Korea—and how these blended harmoniously in Hawaii. The theme of har-

A Bishop Museum exhibit displays Kukailimoku, the feather-covered war god of King Kamehameha the Great. Stick gods are on either side; the sticks below are *kapu (tabu)* sticks, symbol of royalty.

mony is underlined by the inclusion of a number of musical instruments. In smaller cases on various levels are attractively arranged displays from the Museum's extensive collection of necklaces, war clubs, carved images, tools, food bowls, house ornaments, and other artifacts from all over the Pacific. Not only wood and stone, but also shell, bones, teeth, feathers, and plant fibers were ingeniously used by Pacific peoples in making useful and ornamental items.

In the Museum Shop, adjacent to Hawaiian Hall, a large map on one wall shows a generally accepted theory of migration of the Pacific peoples. There are many different theories on this subject, however. As Dr. Force pointed out, "Every anthropologist who tries to trace the course of in-migration in the Pacific tends to draw his arrows with a little different orientation. Our map is intended only to show some notion of the major probable routes."

The map on pages 4 and 5 shows the regions into which the Pacific is traditionally divided. The first and largest division is Polynesia ("Many Islands"), a great triangle about 4,500 miles on a side, with Hawaii, New Zealand, and Easter Island at its three corners. Stretching west of Polynesia and north of the equator, with a small dip below the equator at its eastern end, is Micronesia ("Small Islands"). Below Micronesia, extending westward from Fiji, lies Melanesia ("Black Islands"). Opinions differ on whether or not to include the huge island of New Guinea as part of Melanesia.

The indigenous inhabitants of the three major Pacific regions look somewhat different: Melanesia is so called because most of its people have very dark skin (and usually kinky hair); typical Polynesians are large-framed, brown-skinned, and usually have straight or wavy hair; Micronesians are also brown-skinned and may look like smaller Polynesians. These simple generalizations do not apply to every group or to every individual within an area, and they break down in border regions. Furthermore, on a few islands lying geographically within Micronesia or Melanesia, the inhabitants are essentially Polynesian in both appearance and language.

With one or two minor exceptions, every single habitable island in the entire Pacific was either inhabited or showed signs of previous inhabitation at the time the European explorers arrived on the scene. One theory advanced to account for this thorough saturation, unbelievable in the light of present-day geological knowledge, was that a large mid-Pacific continent called Mu had sunk, leaving its inhabitants clinging to the tops of the higher mountains, which became islands.

The Norwegian anthropologist, Thor Heyerdahl, believes that the Polynesians, at least, were originally American Indians who drifted from South America by raft and paddled from North America by canoe to the Pacific islands. In support of his theory, he constructed a balsa raft, the *Kon-Tiki*, and in 1947, with four other scientific adventurers, succeeded in drifting from Peru to the Tuamotu Archipelago. As one anthropologist with opposing views pointed out, Heyerdahl thereby succeeded in proving that the winds and currents in the Southeast Pacific go in a generally westerly direction, just the way oceanographers always said they did. More particularly, he proved that such a raft voyage *could* have brought people across the Pacific; he did not prove that it actually did. Although Heyerdahl has provided certain additional evidence in support of his theory, more contradictory evidence exists, and the vast majority of Pacific scholars do not accept Heyerdahl's theory. Southeast Asia seems to be the most likely place of origin for the Pacific peoples.

In attempting to solve the complex problem of Pacific migrations, scientists employing a number of approaches are turning up important new information every year. The older physical anthropology, which dealt largely with the external appearance —head shape, eyes, skin, and hair, along with various physical measurements—has been supplemented by new genetic investigations involving such matters as blood types. Archeologists are sifting the debris of centuries-old camp and house sites, studying the development and spread of certain types of artifacts— stone tools, fishhooks, and pottery for example. Radioactive-carbon analysis of bits of charcoal from an ancient fire or discarded bones and shells can provide a reasonably accurate date of occupancy for a site. Religious observances and social patterns and customs, such as those concerning marriage, land control, and political leadership, provide further evidence, as do agricultural practices and the spread of man-introduced plants. Pollen grains from ancient sediments have been studied to establish when certain plants first appeared in an area. Detailed studies of the interrelations among the languages spoken by Pacific peoples are continuing to yield fruitful results.

It is obvious that if man came into the Pacific from Asia, the western islands were probably settled first. During the Ice Age, when the oceans were lower, many of these islands were part of a single land mass or else were separated only by narrow straits which could be crossed in simple dugouts or on rafts. The early immigrants may have included three or more racial stocks (perhaps already somewhat mixed): the short, dark Oceanic Negrito, the pale-skinned Ainoid or Caucasoid, and the brown-skinned Veddoid. Various mixtures of these stocks account for the differences in appearance of the indigenous population found in the various parts of New Guinea and Australia.

The movement from Asia into the unoccupied Southwest Pacific was presumably gradual, starting perhaps as far back as fifty thousand years ago. From one point of view, it has never stopped. But by 16,000 B.C., according to one estimate, man had reached New Guinea. The early inhabitants hunted, fished, and gathered food from wild plants; agriculture was later introduced from Asia. The Indonesians, contributing new genes (including a Mongoloid strain), new languages, and new customs and techniques, were an important group who arrived later. The Oceanic Negroid, who was much larger than the Negrito, may also have been a later arrival, or he may have evolved from the Negrito.

Just when man began to move out to the smaller islands north and east of New Guinea is uncertain. Obviously two things were necessary before such a move was possible: vessels suitable for transoceanic transportation and a knowledge of agricultural techniques to render the islands habitable. Both of these factors may have been introduced by the Indonesians. Perhaps the islands of eastern Melanesia were settled some time between 5000 and 1000 B.C.

Micronesia could have been settled from one or more of three directions: northward from the Bismarck Archipelago, northeastward from the Molucca Islands of Indonesia, or eastward from the Philippines. For these movements, the dates 2000 to 1000 B.C. seem reasonable.

The Polynesians were the greatest seafarers of all. According to one theory, the Polynesians originated as a distinctive people, or "race," somewhere in Southeast Asia and left their homeland either because of war, population pressure, or a desire to travel. Over a relatively few generations, a series of island-hopping moves brought them to western Polynesia, whence they dispersed to the rest of Polynesia. Recently, however, increasing evidence tends to suggest that while the original racial stock came from Asia, perhaps the Polynesian race originated from people living not far west of Polynesia, in eastern Melanesia. Those whose language, culture, and physical traits developed into what we call Polynesian evolved in one direction; those who today live in Melanesia developed in a somewhat different direction, according to this theory.

Certainly, as Dr. Force remarked, we are no longer inclined to believe that "one bright morning a boatload of a hundred people or so set out from Southeast Asia and sailed all the way to Central Polynesia. The migration took many centuries to complete. And the Pacific wasn't a one-way street; across much of it, a back-and-forth process was involved. Storms can blow people off their course; people can move at random in another direction."

Tonga in Western Polynesia was settled somewhere between 1000 and 500 B.C. The islands of Samoa, to the north, were probably settled next. By 100 B.C., according to archeological evidence, the Polynesians were in the Marquesas Islands, well over two thousand miles to the east. Tahiti, which lies between Samoa and the Marquesas, but somewhat to the south, may not have been settled until later. At any rate, by A.D. 1000 all of Central Polynesia, as well as Easter Island in the east and Hawaii in the north, was settled. Perhaps only New Zealand had not been reached by that date. New dates will be given for the inhabitation of the various islands as research continues. In general, dates earlier than those previously accepted are being revealed.

Thus, long before the Atlantic was conquered, the Polynesians, the most amazing mariners in history, sailed across hundreds of miles of the earth's mightiest ocean in vessels whose hulls were hollowed-out trees with various other parts lashed together by ropes and glued or made tight by vegetable gums. The smaller Polynesian sailing craft were single-hulled outrigger canoes; the larger double canoes, their supreme achievement in ocean-going vessels, ranged in length from forty to a hundred feet. The two hulls were joined by crosspieces on which a platform was built to bear one or more small shelters.

Scholars differ as to whether the settling of Polynesia was the result of purposeful voyages of exploration from which the explorers returned to report their discoveries, after which colonizing expeditions went forth, or whether the islands were settled either by travelers who lost their way or by wandering exiles driven from their homes by war or hunger. All of these situations at one time or another doubtless occurred. In any case, the number of voyagers lost at sea must have been large.

The Polynesian navigators had no compasses, but they had a good knowledge of the stars, which would have enabled them to distinguish direction and latitude. Longitude was an unsolved problem—but before the invention of the chronometer, it was also a considerable problem to Europeans. In familiar seas, the Polynesians had a good knowledge of the currents and winds. The presence of an unseen island could have been detected by the sighting of land birds or by cloud formations, reflections of light from the shallow water of a lagoon, or the presence of floating debris. And of course a high island may be seen some distance out to sea.

With them in their canoes the Polynesians brought the food plants they largely depended upon—the taro, banana, coconut, breadfruit, pandanus, yam, sugarcane, and sweet potato. Also they brought their domestic animals: pigs, dogs, and chickens, all used for food. Rats and certain lizards probably went along as stowaways. Except for birds, and in some instances bats, the remote Pacific islands were devoid of higher forms of animal life until the coming of man.

About the plants and animals used by the Polynesians, the greatest controversy has arisen over the sweet potato, the only one which seems to have come from the New World rather than Asia. Dr. Heyerdahl uses the presence of the sweet potato as part of his argument that the Polynesians originated in South America. Scientists who oppose Heyerdahl think it quite possible that the seafaring Polynesians might have made at least one voyage to South America and returned with the sweet potato. Still others deny even that the sweet potato really is a New World plant, and they go so far as to suggest that the Polynesians could have brought it *to* South America.

In the various islands where the Polynesians established themselves, hundreds or even thousands of miles from their most recent point of migration, they developed a number of linguistic, cultural, and even physical variations. Even as French, Italian, Portuguese, and Spanish all grew out of Latin, so Tongan, Samoan, Tahitian, Marquesan, Maori, Hawaiian, and other Polynesian languages presumably had a common source. Although several great gods were universally worshiped throughout most of Polynesia, other gods and demigods were venerated locally. The forms of religious ritual also differed from place to place. The social organization had as its basic unit the extended family (a larger unit than just mother, father, and children). Power resided in chiefs, with the title usually descending through the senior line of the chiefly family. On a large island there might be a number of chiefs, one for each district; complex systems of chiefly rankings developed in some parts of Polynesia. Chiefs were believed to possess *mana,* a supernatural power which commanded great respect.

From where did the Polynesians come to Hawaii? Most likely from the Marquesas, over two thousand miles to the southeast, perhaps about A.D. 750. It seems probable that a second migration came from Tahiti, more directly south of Hawaii, and that from the twelfth to the fourteenth centuries a number of two-way voyages were made along the 2,500-mile route between Tahiti and Hawaii. The name given to the "Big Island," and since then to the state, is a dialectal variation of the legendary Polynesian homeland, Hawaiki. Other islands in Polynesia have essentially the same name—Savai'i in the Samoa group and Havai'i (now called Raiatea) in the Society Islands.

Except for New Zealand, Hawaii afforded the largest land mass in all Polynesia. Here the new settlers flourished and multiplied, developing their own branch of Polynesian culture—their exquisite featherwork and *tapa,* their forms of worship and *tabus,* their stratified social order.

Dr. Force answered a last question: what are the outstanding characteristics and developments of the Pacific cultures? He named three: their manufacture—the wood-carving and weaving, the imprinted *tapa,* and the featherwork unsurpassed anywhere in the world; second, their love of warfare and fighting; and third, richness in the use of language. It is hard for most of us, who are forced to approach their language through translations, to appreciate this aspect. Their everyday language abounds in metaphors and other figures of speech. (A simple example comes to mind, the familiar word *ukulele,* the Hawaiian word for flea. When the ukulele, of Portuguese invention, was introduced, the Hawaiians saw that the nimble fingers of the musician hopped about from fret to fret like fleas, and the similarity provided the name for the new instrument.) And not surprisingly, Dr. Force added that Pacific folklore is as rich as that of any part of the world.

South to Tahiti

Tahiti! Perhaps it is the most glamorous name in the Pacific
—made famous by the art of Gauguin, the writings of Herman
Melville, Charles Nordhoff, James Norman Hall, and Pierre Loti
and spoken of with warmth by seafaring men for two centuries
for its soft climate, its tropical beauty, and its attractive women.
Indeed, Tahiti over the years has become more of a South Sea
ideal than an actual island. But an island it is, the center of
French Polynesia, lying just about as far south of the equator as
Honolulu is north of it.

French Polynesia, embracing much of the southeastern part of
the Polynesian triangle, includes five or more different groups
of islands, totaling about fifteen hundred square miles. To it
belong the high islands of the Marquesas and Society groups,
the smaller groups of the Austral and the Gambier islands, and
the atolls of the Tuamotu Archipelago. Tahiti, in the Society
Islands, possesses more than one-quarter of the land area and
close to two-thirds of the total population of French Polynesia.
The administrative center of the whole region is Tahiti's principal city, Papeete, and one way of telling whether or not a person
knows his way around the Pacific is by his pronunciation of this
city's name. It's Pah-pay-ay'-tay, not Puh-peéty.

Polynesians apparently reached Tahiti, perhaps from the Marquesas, somewhere between A.D. 400 and 700. They established
important centers of Polynesian culture here and on nearby

islands. Their descendants greeted Samuel Wallis, the first European visitor, in 1767.

After a dreadfully hazardous voyage, which involved four months passing through the Strait of Magellan, the wave-weary men aboard Wallis' *Dolphin* were probably no less glad to come upon Tahiti than the original Polynesian settlers had been. Perhaps they were even gladder, for although the Tahitian men seemed inclined to initiate war games which had to be discouraged by the ship's guns, the women were unexpectedly friendly. Since the Tahitians lacked iron, nails came into great demand as items of trade, for obtaining wood, water, and fresh food, as well as for winning the favors of the Tahitian belles. Indeed, the journal of the *Dolphin's* master tells us that the ship's men entered into the trade with such enthusiasm that they pulled out nails and spikes from the ship itself. Strict measures had to be enforced by the officers to keep the ship from being dismantled!

After five weeks in Tahiti, the *Dolphin* continued her long voyage around the world. Eight and a half months later, in 1768, two ships under the French navigator Louis Antoine de Bougainville found Tahiti. He met with a similar welcome, marred somewhat by the fact (which Wallis had also noted) that the Tahitians, with their different ideas of property rights, tended to walk off with any item aboard ship that caught their fancy. Nonetheless, relations between the Tahitians and the French were generally good during the two-week stay, and Bougainville returned with rosy reports of the island paradise. Unfortunately, either the British or the French—or both—seem to have introduced venereal disease into the islands, the first of a number of previously unknown diseases to which the islanders were to fall victim.

Tahiti proved to be a favorite stopping place for the great Captain Cook. After his first stay in 1769, he returned three more times on later voyages to drop anchor in Matavai Bay. Cook's second expedition brought back to England a young Society Islander, Omai, who created quite a sensation among people who had heard of Tahitians but had never seen one.

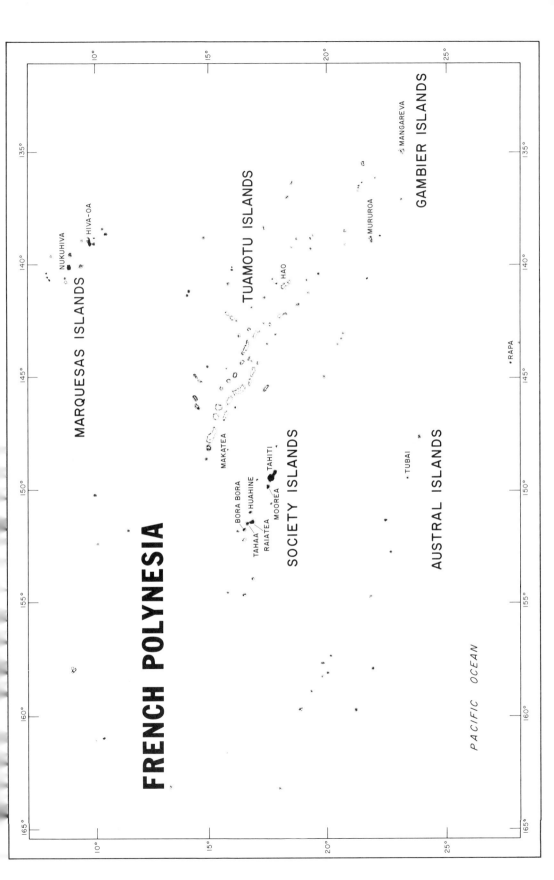

Physically handsome and mild-mannered, he gave much support to the "noble savage" theory—the idea expressed by Rousseau that man in his simple, natural state, unhampered by civilization, was man at his happiest, healthiest, and perhaps best.

Another famous ship to stop at Matavai Bay was the *Bounty* under Captain William Bligh in 1788 and 1789. The British government had decided that the Pacific breadfruit would be a valuable food for their West Indies colonies and sent Bligh's expedition to Tahiti to obtain some young trees. Bligh lost the *Bounty* in the historic mutiny, but returned in 1792 in another ship to carry out his mission.

The desire to convert such noble savages as Omai to Christianity resulted in Tahiti's being chosen as the site for the first Protestant missionary work in the Pacific. The ship *Duff* brought a small group of missionaries of the London Missionary Society in 1797.

The large end of Tahiti may be seen from the small end, across the bay.

Before the coming of the Europeans, the Society Islands were controlled by a number of chiefs, with several high chiefs on Tahiti alone. As was true elsewhere in the Pacific islands, the introduction of firearms enabled one chief to amass sufficient power to obtain control over a large island, and eventually over an entire group of islands. The missionaries, who were used to a political system involving a single king, also contributed to this process of unification by supporting a single chief as sovereign.

In Tahiti such a chief was Tu, later known as Pomare, who in 1790, with the aid of the weapons from the *Bounty* mutineers, began the conquest of all Tahiti. His successors, Pomare II and Pomare III, were followed by a queen, Pomare IV, who ruled for half a century, from 1827 to 1877. Although the islands were independent at the start of her rule, the missionaries exerted a strong British influence. The expulsion of the first French Roman Catholic missionaries in the late 1830's brought French naval forces and the threat of a military take-over. After about ten years of unsettled conditions, including some fighting, Pomare IV finally accepted French Protectorate status in 1847. Upon the abdication of Pomare's son, Pomare V, who ruled from 1877 to 1880, Tahiti became a French colony.

Most of the other islands of French Polynesia also came officially under French control during the 1880's. Today, except for residents of foreign descent, the inhabitants of French Polynesia are French citizens and send both an elected deputy and a senator to the French parliament. Although there is also an elected Territorial Assembly, the regional governor is not elected but appointed.

Tahiti was formed by two volcanoes, and the resulting 400-square-mile island looks like a lopsided figure eight. The large western end, rising to over 7,300 feet, is joined to the smaller 4,400-foot-high eastern end by a narrow peninsula. Erosion has cut deep narrow valleys down the sides of the original volcanoes, and large central depressions surrounded by peaks mark the original craters. Around most of the island lies a line of cliffs or steep slopes a hundred or more feet high. A relatively narrow strip of flat land—rarely more than half a mile wide—lies between their bases and the ocean. Most of the eighty thousand or more people on the island live either along this strip or in the mouths of the valleys. The rugged inland is rarely visited; in fact, parts of it are considered still unexplored.

The lack of flat land has made large-scale agriculture, such as sugarcane plantations, unfeasible for Tahiti. For a long while, it also prohibited air transportation to the island except by seaplane. A 12,000-foot runway was finally completed, however, on Tahiti's reef in the district of Faaa (pronounce each *a* separately), three miles from Papeete. The jet age came to Tahiti in 1961; terminal facilities for an international airport followed.

Today Tahiti has a variety of peoples although Polynesians predominate. Unlike Hawaiian, Tahitian is obviously a living language. But there is a good deal of French in the air, too, and most residents of Tahiti, whether European, Chinese, or Polynesian, are fluent in both languages. With the influx of American travelers, English is increasingly being used as a third language, and many signs are in all three languages.

Tahitians dress informally in Western style most of the time, wearing colorful sport shirts and dresses. More traditional Polynesian costumes are worn by Tahitian singers and dancers. Unlike Hawaiians, Tahitians are not known for the excellence of their flower leis; they do excel in a wide variety of beautiful leis made from shells, and in fern and flower coronets made fresh each day which the women and many of the men wear on their heads. The sweet smell of the *tiare Tahiti*, a gardenia woven into many of these headdresses, fills the air.

A good many Pacific islands must guard against the arrival of outsiders who have barely enough money to get there but who have visions of staying, plucking native fruits or coconuts for food, and living an idyllic life with little or no work—perhaps becoming beachcombers. Actually, the real era of the Pacific beachcomber, a man from another society who lived with and adopted the customs of a native society, was essentially over by 1850. To call every unemployed outsider a beachcomber is to give him a title he does not deserve. But the islands need to be protected against having to support tropical tramps, and so most island governments require that a visitor either have a return ticket or deposit an equivalent sum of money with a local bank or travel agency. In French Polynesia, passports and visas are also required; no non-French citizen can stay longer than six months without special permission. Even temporary employment is not usually permitted to a visitor.

Tahitian dancing, which is performed at various public and private events and at the tourist hotels, is not the soft swaying of Hawaiian dancers; it is, good-humoredly and frankly—but unobjectionably—sexual in its underlying meaning. And its tempo is fast. No other Polynesian dancer can get such rapid vibration of the hips into a dance as a Tahitian woman—unless possibly it is a Tahitian man! The typical female native-style costume worn by dancers may consist of an ankle-length grass skirt with a bra top; the males wear a somewhat shorter skirt and no top. As a compromise the skirt may be a more modern wrap-

A crown of flowers and ferns is the favorite Tahitian adornment.

around of *pareu* cloth, a bright cotton print which Tahitians use for shirts, skirts, dresses, or curtains.

No less interesting than the dancers' performance is that of the accompanying musicians, especially the drummers, who pound out their rhythms on a large hollowed-out tree trunk, several smaller hollow blocks of wood, and a five-gallon tin can. The staccato patterns of these various drums are different, interweaving intricately as they meet and separate.

At a *tamaaraa,* or native feast, music and dancing are the principal entertainments; pork is the chief dish. Particulary delicious is Tahitian raw fish prepared in a marinade of lime juice mellowed with coconut milk. Where the Hawaiian *poi* is a paste of cooked taro, the Tahitian *poe* is more like a pudding with fruit —banana, papaya, or whatever is available.

One can travel around Tahiti on his own, either on foot, by renting a car, or on a local bus (called *le truck*) with hard wooden benches, packed with people, produce, chickens, pigs, bags, and cartons. Papeete is an interesting town with over thirty thousand inhabitants. A busy street curves around the rim of the harbor, and the town's center extends back from the waterfront for several blocks. While naval and cargo ships usually use the newer piers, the most interesting craft—the cruise ships and the yachts—tie up along the old waterfront.

A block away from the waterfront, behind a park, stand the new government buildings and the former site of Pomare's palace. Not far away is Papeete's small museum. The public market, which occupies a whole block, is the town's most interesting gathering place. Here tropical produce and fish are sold and the latest gossip exchanged.

Many of the businesses along Papeete's streets are operated by Chinese, of whom there are over ten thousand in French Polynesia. No new immigrants from China have been allowed for several decades, but children born of Chinese parents in French Polynesia are considered citizens of Nationalist China until they have formally gained French citizenship.

At the north end of Papeete, Fautaua Valley leads to Bain Loti, Loti's Pool. Pierre Loti, a distinguished French writer who traveled widely during his more than forty years as cadet and officer in the French navy, made perhaps the most important contribution to the romantic legend of Tahiti in *The Marriage of Loti*. This semi-autobiographical novel deals with a young naval officer's stay in Tahiti in the 1870's and his love affair with a teenaged Tahitian, Rarahu. Many of the book's episodes deal with the meetings of the two lovers at their private bath, a pool in the Fautaua stream. A small monument to Loti stands by a pool in the deep gorge.

Papeete and its surrounding areas are changing. Fortunately, the new business buildings so far are all two to four stories high, following a general height which one writer expressed as "two-thirds of a coconut tree." Tahiti's new hotels, built on the water outside Papeete proper, are mostly low-rise, although one of them is seven stories high. Another, with actually nine or ten stories, is built stepwise down the side of a hill, so that in any one place it is no more than two or three floors above the land.

About seven miles from Papeete is Matavai Bay, the historic anchorage of Wallis, Cook, and Bligh. Beyond the bay is Pointe Venus, so named not because of the beauty of the Tahitian maidens, but because Cook set up his astronomical observatory there to observe the passage of the planet Venus across the sun in 1769. On the point are a garden, a monument, and a "living museum" honoring the discoverers of Tahiti. On the bay side of the point, Tahitian children frolic in the water off a beach which, like many in Tahiti, is largely black sand.

One may continue around the large end of the island and head back toward Papeete along the south side. Just beyond the "neck" of the island, the road passes a large botanical garden in which stands the Gauguin Museum, opened in 1964 in honor of the great French artist who, after reading Loti's account of Polynesian life, spent about ten years in Tahiti and the Marquesas. His life was a constant struggle to keep out of debt. Today one of his paintings is worth hundreds of thousands of dollars, and his primitivistic, brightly hued South Sea works are recognized the world over. So valuable are Gauguin paintings that the Gauguin Museum cannot afford to buy one. Nonetheless, the building—itself a notable example of modern architecture—contains many excellent reproductions of his work as well as photographs, newspaper items, and documents concerning his life.

Throughout French Polynesia are many old *maraes*, or native temples. The ruins of the huge Marae Mahaiatea, visited by Captain Cook, lie between the main road and the shore. Once one of the biggest structures in Polynesia, it is now less imposing because many of its stones were used for road building and other construction after the conversion of the Tahitians to Christianity. Nearer Papeete, Marae Arahurahu lies inland from the road in the mouth of a valley. It consists of a large rectangular stone enclosure three or four feet high in the center of which, surrounded by grass, the main temple structure rises

On Pointe Venus, Captain Cook made astronomical observations during his first trip to Tahiti.

The Gauguin Museum honors the greatest artist of the South Seas.

to a height of about fifteen feet in three successively shorter tiers. All of the stones in the walls seem to be stream-rounded boulders of about the same size, and, at a glance, it looks as if the Tahitians miraculously succeeded in building perpendicular walls out of cannonballs without mortar.

Marae Arahurahu has been restored even to the extent of having several carved images on posts within the enclosure and is well kept by the *marae*-keeper, who lives in a truly native house a few yards up the valley. A narrow but well-defined trail leads beyond his house through coffee, banana, and coconut groves. Coffee was once considered a potentially important crop on the island and small quantities were exported, but today almost all that is grown is used locally. The trail winds back and forth across the valley stream; here and there stand walls once used for house sites or perhaps for taro terraces.

From Tahiti, a DC-4 flies to Bora Bora, one of the five high islands which lie west of Tahiti and Moorea, in the Leeward group of the Society Islands. Soon after taking off, the plane flies over the bays and pinnacles of Moorea, Tahiti's nearest neighbor. A hundred miles farther west, the plane pauses at Raiatea, second largest of the Society Islands, which stands beside its smaller neighbor, Tahaa, within a single reef. Both Raiatea and nearby Huahine have many ancient ruins. Dr. Yosihiko Sinoto, a Bishop Museum archeologist working on a French government project, has supervised the restoration of twenty-nine *marae*s on the two islands.

Raiatea—formerly named Havai'i or Havaiki, perhaps after a still older Polynesian island—may have been the original center of dispersal for much of central and southern Polynesia. Tradition has it that a fleet of canoes set forth from here in the fourteenth century and found New Zealand. Today Raiatea is one of the several Society Islands making a bid for tourist business.

In an ocean full of breathtakingly beautiful islands, Bora Bora is, as James Michener has said, "considered by most judges to be the most beautiful in the world." Michener's own delight in Bora Bora's beauty was perhaps one reason he chose to use "wild, impetuous, lovely Bora Bora" as the starting point for the migration of the Hawaiians in his novel *Hawaii.*

It is an irregularly shaped island, six miles long and two and a half miles wide, with bays and peninsulas along its perimeter. In its center, twin-peaked Mount Pahia rises to 2,165 feet, and Mount Temanu, a dramatic block of basalt with sheer cliffs on its sides, extends two hundred feet higher. The steep slopes of the central mountains become more gentle toward sea level, and a flat region stretches along the coast. The main island and a pair of islets which were also once part of the original volcano are entirely surrounded by a barrier reef which encloses a striking emerald-and-blue lagoon that averages a mile in width. On the north and east sides, a number of low, wooded islets rest atop the reef's outer edge. A single pass through the reef leads to the deep natural harbor of the lagoon, where cruise ships can anchor when ferrying their passengers to the island in small boats.

The plane lands at an airfield built by American forces during World War II on a reef island at the north end of the lagoon.

Several launches wait to carry passengers and baggage to the principal village, Vaitape, on the main island.

A few days' stay on Bora Bora is very rewarding. Tourism is growing and there are two good—and expanding—hotels. The lagoon offers water skiing, outrigger-canoe sailing, scuba diving, snorkeling, or simply swimming in water which has a color so unbelievable it ought to be sold by the bottle. Motorcycles and a few cars offer transportation, but on such a small island bicycles are very practical. Nobody seems to care much whether a bicycle's tires hold air or whether the vehicle has much of a seat left, as long as it pedals.

On a tour around the island the lagoon and mountains provide scenic features for most of the trip, with fruit trees, gardens, and coconut groves along the flat land and up the slopes. Several *marae*s stand near the road; on Bora Bora they are constructed of large slabs of coral from the reef rather than of rocks from streams, for Bora Bora has no large permanent streams.

The Polynesians here, like the people in the rural regions of Tahiti, seem more friendly than the sophisticated town-dwellers of Papeete, and they greet strangers with an *"'Ia ora na."* Here, too, more of the dwellings are of Polynesian construction, elevated on short posts with sides of plaited strips of bamboo or other material and thatched pandanus leaf roofs. *Pareu* cloth curtains hang in the windows. Although a house may sit in a yard surrounded by a hedge, the usual yard has a simple surface of clean-swept sand, not grass.

On a hill overlooking the lagoon old naval guns of Spanish-American War vintage were set up by the Americans in the 1940's to defend Bora Bora's strategically important harbor. They still point out toward the pass in the reef, to the right of which stands Motu Tapu (Sacred Island), a little gem of a reef island that was used for the setting of an early South Sea movie. The hill offers a good view of much of beautiful Bora Bora and makes one wonder whether tourism will spoil the island. Perhaps not; the American military establishment there during the war didn't.

Another scenic island, Moorea, beckons spectacularly across

the water from Tahiti. Although small planes serve as taxis, most people cross the twelve-mile strait from Tahiti to Moorea aboard one of the daily launches, a trip of less than two hours. The launch, a broad-beamed vessel more than fifty feet long, carries assorted cargo on its roofed-over rear deck—fuel drums, cases of beer, cartons of canned goods, motorcycles, and passengers. Though the trip is not long, the channel can be a threat to those with sensitive stomachs. The usual clouds provide a backdrop for the spires, pinnacles, and ramparts of Moorea's fantastic 4,000-foot mountains which were created by erosion from a huge volcano, older than the ones which formed Tahiti. The launch docks in Paopao (Cook) Bay, a deep indentation extending back several miles from the pass through the reef. Just to its right is Mount Rotui; farther in the background the jagged 2,950-foot peak of Mouaroa boldly spears the sky.

Since the launch will return in five hours, there will be time

The jagged peaks of Moorea as viewed from Tahiti make a picture of timeless beauty.

only for a lunch at one of Moorea's several hotels, which enjoy a thriving tourist trade, and a thirty-seven-mile drive around the island. Moorea's population, now approaching five thousand, is predominately Polynesian. The sights are similar to those on Tahiti and Bora Bora—copra plantations, vanilla plantations, banana groves, coffee and grapefruit trees, pineapples, small villages with Chinese-operated general stores, thatched-roofed dwellings (and some larger houses used as vacation retreats by the wealthy), and several notable churches, the oldest dating back to 1829. As one heads back to Papeete, Tahiti's huge bulk across the water presents a relatively featureless and uninteresting profile after a circuit of Moorea's dramatically pointed peaks.

The rest of French Polynesia is interesting, but difficult to visit. Between three and six hundred miles to the south and southwest of Tahiti lie the remote Austral Islands, five of which are inhabited, with a total population in 1971 of 5,079 on their fifty-five or sixty square miles. They are geologically high islands, the summits of submerged mountains which rise from 315 to 2,077 feet above the sea. The Austral Islands are visited at intervals by small ships which bring supplies and carry off their exports—native handicraft, pigs, cattle, copra, vanilla, and other crops—to Papeete. Subsistence agriculture, however, is the chief activity.

Rapa, the farthest south of the Austral Islands, has too cold a climate for breadfruit or coconuts. The tribes which originally inhabited this mountainous island conducted continual warfare, principally for control of the best agricultural land. To protect themselves against unexpected attacks, the Rapans built fortified villages on the peaks of steep mountain ridges. The earth and stone remains of these forts still command Rapa's heights. With the coming of missionaries and whalers, the warfare ceased, but the population, once two thousand, died off rapidly from diseases introduced there, until in 1863 fewer than a hundred and fifty people remained. In 1967 the population was reported as 363, almost all of them Polynesian.

To the east of Tahiti nearly eighty islands of the far-flung

Tuamotu Archipelago extend for about a thousand miles in a belt which runs in a generally southeasterly direction. Also called the Paumotu or Low Archipelago, the islands are, with one exception, atolls, several of them nearly a hundred miles in circumference. Because their waters are filled with dangerous reefs and treacherous currents, the islands have still a fourth name, the Dangerous Archipelago, which was given them by Bougainville. Dozens of ships have been wrecked or have disappeared here. About thirty of the atolls are entirely uninhabited; on the other islands there are between six and seven thousand people who live off fish, chickens, coconuts, breadfruit, bananas, pandanus, and, on some islands, papayas, melons, and taro. Imported foods (rice, flour, and canned goods), cloth, and other necessary items are brought in by trading schooners which carry away copra, the principal item of commerce.

In the last half of the nineteenth century, pearl shell, removed from island lagoons by Tuamotan divers who went to depths of over a hundred feet with only a pair of goggles, was an important export. With luck, pearls were sometimes found in a few of the oysters. The introduction of diving equipment caused a rapid depletion of the oyster resources. Today diving machines are illegal, and the industry is regulated to preserve the supply, but the demand is not as great as it once was.

Near the northwest end of the Tuamoto Archipelago is Makatea, which differs from the other Tuamotuan islands in that it is constructed of uplifted coral reaching a height of 372 feet above sea level. Scientists use its name to describe other islands of this type that occur elsewhere in the Pacific. About five miles long and two miles wide, it lacks a harbor and is generally less habitable than some of the atolls. Yet for nearly sixty years, from 1908 to 1966, this small island was the most important economic resource in all of French Polynesia, for in its interior were rich deposits of phosphate rock. Two to three hundred thousand tons were dug out annually by imported laborers. In 1966, when the supply was exhausted, the plant closed down and the miners left.

France, which did not sign the international nuclear test ban treaty in 1963, has used several uninhabited islands in the eastern Tuamotus for nuclear weapon tests. Mururoa Atoll, about seven hundred and fifty miles from Tahiti, was chosen as the site of the actual detonations, including hydrogen bomb blasts. Tests in 1970 and 1971 drew protests from many Pacific countries.

At the far eastern end of the Tuamotu Archipelago is another small cluster of islands, the Mangareva or Gambier islands, which consist of four high inhabited islands and several smaller islets, in a lagoon surrounded by a barrier reef with a circumference of forty miles. This lagoon provided a safe harbor for whalers and other sailing vessels led to it by the sharp peak of 1,447-foot Mount Duff. Once the home of several thousand people, these islands today have fewer than six hundred inhabitants.

The Gambiers were the scene of early French Catholic missionary work, and the principal settlement contains a huge white coral cathedral easily capable of seating the entire population. Mangareva (the largest island in the group) is the administrative center not only for the Gambier Islands but also for some of the eastern Tuamotus. In 1968, in connection with the atomic tests two hundred miles away, the French completed a 7,200-foot airstrip in the Gambiers. Future use of this facility by commercial planes will reduce Mangareva's isolation and make tourism possible.

Seven hundred and forty miles to the northeast of Tahiti, beyond the Tuamotus, lie the Marquesas Islands, the second largest group of high islands in French Polynesia and possibly the first group in the area to be settled by Polynesians. The islands are about 250 miles from one end to the other and contain between 450 and 500 square miles of land. The two largest, Nuku Hiva and Hiva Oa, are each over 125 square miles in area.

The story of the depopulation and cultural devastation of this exceptionally beautiful island group is one of the most tragic tales of the Pacific. Mendaña discovered the islands in 1595, and several hundred Marquesans were slaughtered by the guns of the Spaniards during the explorer's two-week stay. Mendaña named his discovery Las Islas Marquesas de Mendoza after the viceroy of Peru. The handsome Polynesians drew considerable attention, and the Marquesan women were favorably compared with the beautiful women of Lima.

Following their first unhappy contact with European civilization, the Marquesans carried on their private wars and practiced their arts of tattooing, wood carving, and stone carving with little outside interference until late in the eighteenth century. On the larger islands, the various tribes were frequently at war with their neighbors. On occasion, at least part of a slain warrior was undoubtedly eaten by his conquerors. Some form of cannibalism was practiced on many of the Pacific Islands, often as a ritual—perhaps following a battle, either as a display of supreme contempt for the enemy or in an attempt to acquire some of the slain foe's power. In very few areas—mostly in Melanesia, but possibly in the Marquesas—was human flesh looked upon as food.

Captain Cook rediscovered the islands and stayed a few days on his second voyage in the 1770's. In 1791 the first American merchant vessel passed the Marquesas, and during the next fifty years it was a favorite provisioning and recreation point for other trading ships and merchant vessels and for the whaling ships that swarmed the Pacific. The Marquesans died rapidly from the firearms which some of the chiefs had obtained from the sailors, but even more died of diseases introduced by Europeans. The population, which may well have been over 100,000 in 1790, was only about 20,000 fifty years later, and it continued to drop.

Among the many whaling ships that dropped anchor in Taiohae Bay at Nuku Hiva, one bore a seaman in his early twenties, Herman Melville. Dissatisfied with conditions aboard his ship, the *Acushnet*, Melville and a companion decided to jump ship when the vessel paused at Nuku Hiva in July of 1842. He spent an exciting four weeks living with a rather remote and uncivilized tribe in the Taipi Valley. This experience formed the basis for Melville's first book, *Typee*, published in 1846.

Melville's book really marks the beginning of Pacific literature. It contains a number of elements that make thrilling reading—the escape from the ship, the hair-raising descent of a mountain, life with a primitive people who have strange customs, a tenderhearted Polynesian maiden, the threat of cannibalism, and the final escape from the tribe, which jealously tries to prevent his leaving.

The French navy moved in to control the Marquesas in 1842, and the islands had the status of a French protectorate until they were formally proclaimed a colony in 1880. A French Catholic mission was established in the late 1830's. The early missionaries were quite friendly and understanding in their dealings with the Marquesans; later missionaries introduced strict measures, abolishing native dress, dances, songs, religious practices, and tattooing—in effect, wiping out most of the indigenous culture.

Attempts were made to introduce large-scale agriculture, particularly cattle raising and cotton growing. Many of the cattle went wild and their descendants are still hunted today; cotton production ceased over half a century ago. Chinese labor was imported to work on a large cotton plantation, but the plantation failed. The opium habit, introduced in that period, may have contributed, along with the already introduced taste for alcohol, to the decline of the Marquesans.

The population continued to drop, to about four thousand by the end of the century. The famous author-yachtsman Robert Louis Stevenson, who visited the Marquesas in 1888, and Jack London, who called aboard his *Snark* in 1907, visited Melville's Taipi Valley and were horrified at the changes that had taken place. Where once thousands of healthy, energetic (and at times ferocious) Marquesans had lived, there remained a pitiful handful of sickly, dazed people looking forward to a bleak future. The huge dancing plaza, six hundred feet long, the largest in Polynesia, was vacant and overgrown. Much of the agriculturally rich valley and its house sites had reverted to a tangle, through which buzzed swarms of a particularly pesky biting fly.

The end of the Marquesans was predicted. In the 1920's and 1930's, the population dropped until there were fewer than fifteen hundred Marquesans, about one percent of the original number. But there has been an increase since then, and today more than fifty-five hundred inhabitants live on these rarely visited islands. Copra production is their chief source of cash.

What is the future of French Polynesia? Economically, the islands have exhausted what was once their greatest money-maker, the phosphate from Makatea. This leaves copra, of which two or three million dollars' worth is shipped annually from all the islands, as the chief export. The value of vanilla, the next most important crop, is about half as much. Vanilla, actually the

A mat-sized hat is woven of pandanus leaves. Tourism is an important economic resource.

fragrant pod of a climbing orchid, brings a high price per pound but requires a great amount of tedious hand labor. Its cultivation is a small-scale industry, usually carried on in family plots. Pearl shell and handicrafts are smaller exports.

Tourism is already bringing in much more money than phosphate ever did. In 1970 the number of visitors, not including cruise-ship passengers, was nearly fifty thousand, and predictions are that there may be a quarter of a million by 1976. This increase in numbers will doubtless effect many changes, but as far back as the 1830's people were writing that the old Tahiti had been ruined by outsiders. For some time, tourism will continue to be concentrated in the Society Islands; the inhabitants of the other groups will benefit only very indirectly from any resulting prosperity.

The population of French Polynesia is now increasing almost everywhere, having grown from a total of 44,000 in 1936 to 84,000 in 1962. Today it has passed 110,000—still fewer, no doubt, than before the coming of the Europeans.

What about the political future of French Polynesia? Other regions of the Pacific have moved to independence, or to a greater degree of self-government, as colonies have become obsolete. Since World War II, France has greatly reorganized its former empire, granting independence to many of its colonies or protectorates. In 1958 each of the remaining French-governed areas outside Europe was given a choice of becoming independent or remaining with France, either as a *département* (politically like a part of European France) or as an "overseas territory" (presumably with a little more self-government). France's three Pacific colonies—French Polynesia, New Caledonia, and Wallis and Futuna—chose to remain French territories.

Although the 1958 decision presumably settled French Polynesia's political future, the citizens have not been entirely happy with their status. They are under a governor appointed by the central government in France, not elected by the people. Elections are conducted for such bodies as the Territorial Assembly and certain municipal councils, and the island of Tahiti has four elected mayors. But in recent years the great majority of successful candidates for elected office have been people who are strongly in favor of more autonomy for French Polynesia. It seems evident that French Polynesia would like the privilege of electing its own governor, at least; for reasons of practical economics, complete independence has fewer supporters. Since sixty percent of the cost of running French Polynesia comes out of the French national budget, most businessmen feel that the territorial government does not at present have the resources to "go it alone." Attempts to replace the contribution of the French government by increased local taxes have met with unexpectedly violent opposition.

One French national custom the Polynesians have wholeheartedly adopted is an all-out celebration of Bastille Day, July

On Bastille Day, July 14, crowds gather in Papeete for festivities.

14, France's national holiday. Athletic contests, parades, music, dancing, feasting, and a general carnival atmosphere continue not just for the day, but for a week or two. Everybody from the whole island of Tahiti crowds the Papeete streets, made smaller by dozens of little booths which spring up as if by magic. If French Polynesia ever becomes independent, there would have to be an annual Independence Day celebration to replace Bastille Day.

The French Territory of Wallis and Futuna, although it lies on the western fringe of Polynesia, is a separate territory, not part of French Polynesia. Its three major islands contain about sixty square miles of land. Wallis Island, also called Uvea, lies 1,800 miles west of Papeete. It consists of one good-sized volcanic island which rises to 470 feet above sea level and is surrounded by a barrier reef which includes over twenty other islets. Futuna, 100 miles to the southwest, is a higher island (half a mile high) of about the same area as Wallis, with only a fringing reef. Across a two-mile channel lies its half-size neighbor, Alofi.

The nine thousand people living in Wallis and Futuna engage in subsistence agriculture and copra production, although the huge rhinoceros beetle, a serious pest in some parts of the Pacific, has greatly affected the copra crop. Another large group of Wallis and Futuna people—perhaps five thousand—have emigrated elsewhere, principally to the Melanesian islands of New Caledonia and the New Hebrides.

American Samoa

A flight from Tahiti to American Samoa, 1,400 miles to the west, passes between the two groups of the Cook Islands, though they are too far away to be seen. They include fifteen widely separated islands stretching about a thousand miles from north to south, with a total area of nearly one hundred square miles and a population of 20,000. The eight islands of the southern Cooks include a half dozen of volcanic origin, with hills or mountains in the center; the northern Cooks are small atolls, the largest of which has a lagoon fourteen miles across.

The Cook Islands were taken under British protection late in the nineteenth century, and early in the present century became a part of New Zealand. Since 1964 they have had full self-government in free association with New Zealand, which is responsible for their external affairs and defense. The Cook Islanders possess common citizenship with New Zealanders, and thousands of Cook Islanders go to New Zealand to live and work, some returning after a few years. New Zealand is also the principal market for the citrus, tomatoes, coffee, bananas, pineapples, and fruit juice produced in the southern Cooks. The northern Cooks produce copra and pearl shell.

Rarotonga, a beautiful twenty-six-square-mile island with several mountains over two thousand feet tall, is the center of government and commerce. Cruise ships often stop there, although the harbor is too small for such ships to enter. However,

Rarotonga has plans for developing a tourist industry; the New Zealand government is building an international jet airport.

The high islands of the Samoa group, inhabited by a single branch of Polynesians, stretch 250 miles from east to west. The western islands, including the two largest, Savai'i and Upolu, form the independent country of Western Samoa; the smaller eastern islands are an unincorporated territory of the United States. Western Samoa has nearly 1,100 square miles of land area and a population approaching 150,000; American Samoa has only 76 square miles and a population of about 25,000.

The Samoas were first sighted by the Dutch captain Roggeveen in 1722, and in 1768 they were visited by Bougainville, who named them the Navigators' Islands, because of the large number of skillfully handled canoes he saw in the islands' waters. Another Frenchman, La Pérouse, stopped for water at what is now American Samoa in 1787 and engaged in a bloody battle with the Samoans in which a dozen Frenchmen were killed. From 1790 on, various exploring ships and an increasing number of whalers and traders stopped at the islands.

During this period, the islands were controlled by a number of rival chiefs who conducted frequent and extensive wars. Although at times a single chief emerged as king of the entire group, Samoa was unable to establish a stable dynasty such as that of the Pomares in Tahiti or the Kamehamehas in Hawaii. The London Missionary Society began work in Samoa in 1830, although native missionaries from Tonga had arrived a few years earlier.

The three powers which were to have the most to do with Samoa's future—Britain, Germany, and the United States—began to show interest in Samoa in the middle of the nineteenth century. Britain and Germany appointed consuls in Samoa; the United States named a commercial agent. As political rivalry between Samoan chiefs continued, the representatives of the three major powers, and the missionaries as well, often became involved in local disputes in attempts to end the warfare and stabilize the government.

During a particularly heated struggle in 1888, foreign naval vessels began arriving at Samoa: the British and Americans supported one Samoan faction and the Germans another. A war might have broken out had not a hurricane occurred on March 16, 1889. Of the seven warships present, the three American ships and the three German ships were driven ashore and wrecked; the single British ship managed to escape. Several months later, at a conference in Berlin, the powers agreed to declare Samoa neutral. Rebellions continued, however, and in 1899 a new treaty put Eastern Samoa under American control and Western Samoa under the control of the other two nations. Almost immediately, Britain traded her share of Samoa to Germany in exchange for rights in Tonga and several of the Solomon Islands.

Lying on the western edge of Polynesia, Samoa was one of the first areas settled by Polynesians, probably at least three centuries before Christ, and it may have been the place from which settlers of other Polynesian islands to the east departed. It is also a region which, while adopting Christianity and certain aspects of Western-style government, has clung tenaciously to many of the old social customs. Samoans take a fierce pride in doing things *fa'a Samoa*—the Samoan way. And it is the region where Polynesians are increasing numerically at the greatest rate; population control may well be the Samoans' greatest future problem.

Because of Samoa's warmth and humidity, a specialized native-style dwelling evolved to provide the best possible ventilation—an oval house, or *fale*, which has no real walls, but consists of a ring of posts around the outer edges and a very high thatched roof supported in the center by one or more posts. Woven mats, usually rolled up under the eaves, can be lowered to keep out wind and rain or for privacy, though Samoans live their private lives pretty much in public.

There are no partitions or closets; articles not needed are stored up among the rafters. The smaller *fale*s are only a few inches off the ground; a sill consisting of lengths of tree trunk or large stones separates the inside from the outside. The outside yard is gravel; the inside is usually flat pebbles covered with

A typical *fale*, or village house. This one is actually located in Western Samoa.

mats. The larger houses of important people stand on walled structures which may rise five or six feet above the ground. The big Samoan buildings for ceremonies or meetings have the same architecture, though they may be round rather than oval.

The island of Tutuila in American Samoa has the only large airport in the islands; it was enlarged for jet planes in the early 1960's. The modern airport buildings follow the old Samoan architecture as closely as possible. The Pago Pago Interconti-nental Hotel, about eight miles away, also follows generally Samoan-type architecture—but it does have walls!

In pronouncing Samoan, as in all Polynesian languages, one must remember to sound all vowels with a Romance-language (*ah, eh, ee, oh, oo*) vowel sound. What is troublesome here and in some of the other Polynesian islands, is the *ng* sound. The problem is increased by the fact that the missionaries who first put the language into writing used a *g* for the *ng* sound. Thus, Pago Pago is really Pango Pango. But how do you pronounce *Pango*? Not as if it rhymed with *tango*, though one hears many travelers doing this. For a close approximation, say *pong* (as in *ping-pong*) and immediately follow it with an *o* sound. Not *Pong-go*; get that extra *g* out of there—just *Pong-o*.

The road from the airport to the hotel passes a number of *fale*s, and since there are no walls one can clearly see the people in each house going about their business. Although some houses contain chairs and beds, floor mats often serve the purpose of either or both. Cooking is done not in the *fale*, but in a small cook-shed nearby. Unfortunately, many of the *fale*s in American Samoa have rather unattractive galvanized metal roofs, often installed on top of the more picturesque thatching. Actually they're more practical—they last longer and are less likely to develop leaks. To weigh the roofs down in case of high winds, the Samoans often use old tires, in pairs joined by a rope with

Tutuila rises steeply from the Pacific, with little level land along much of its coast.

one tire resting on the front side of the roof and the other on the back. At a quick glance, it looks as if the home owner may be afraid of a tidal wave and has his life preservers on the rooftop ready for high water.

Samoa is subject to occasional hurricanes, to which native-style houses are especially vulnerable. In 1966 a particularly bad hurricane destroyed a large number of *fales*. Federal funds helped in the building of 650 relief homes, many of which are evident along the road. Federally-financed houses must meet certain standards, and the resulting structures have changed American Samoa's appearance. They are rectangular, not oval, and while they have the one room typical of Samoan houses, they have slab floors, which the *fales* do not. Although they have many large, nearly full-length, open windows, they have complete walls at the corners and shingled roofs which are less sharply pitched than those of the old *fales*.

The hotel, completed in the mid-1960's, partly with local capital in a bid for increased tourism, sits on a point which projects into Pago Pago harbor, one of the finest and most beautiful in the Pacific. Across the harbor rise three or four high peaks, including the 1,700-foot-high "Rainmaker"—so called because the average annual rainfall near the harbor is about 190 inches per year. The harbor (a bay about a mile and a half long which nearly cuts the narrow island in half) provides a center for commercial activity; around its edges are a number of villages. The village of Pago Pago itself lies at the head of the bay; the real commercial and government center of the island is nearby Fagatogo (did you remember to pronounce those *g*'s as *ng*'s?).

The excellence of Pago Pago harbor and its usefulness as a coaling station first drew American interest in 1872, although America did not actually establish a naval base there until after obtaining Eastern Samoa in 1899. For half a century, American Samoa was administered by the United States Navy, not entirely without periods of unrest among the Samoans. In 1951, the administration was turned over to the Department of the Interior, and the islands were given their present status. American Samoa has a Senate, made up of fifteen traditional high chiefs, and a House of Representatives, consisting of seventeen elected members. A governor is appointed by the President.

Samoa's social system is a specialized version of the social systems existing—or formerly existing—elsewhere in Polynesia. The basic unit of society is the *aiga*, an extended family (more like a clan than a Western family), including a number of individuals related not only by blood but by marriage or adoption. Every family has two chiefs—a chief and a talking chief—each of whom has certain functions and privileges. Essentially, one might say the talking chief acts as the executive officer of the chief. Either kind of chief is called a *matai*. A *matai*'s position depends on his being acknowledged as head by the members of the *aiga*, not on inheritance, though often a *matai* is the son of a previous *matai*. There may be a total of ten thousand chiefs in American and Western Samoa.

A *matai* has control of the family's land, property, economy, and general welfare and is the most important agent in establishing or maintaining a family's prestige. Prestige is particularly indicated by the magnitude of feasts and ceremonies on important occasions. The *matai* of a village are the members of the village council, which meets frequently to discuss village affairs. Some of the *matai* may also sit in a larger council of a sub-district or district.

Under the *matai* system, an individual's responsibility is to his *aiga*, not to himself. Strictly speaking, a person does not really "own" any personal property; it is family property, and any member of the *aiga* is entitled to help himself to it or use it for as long as he wants. In theory at least, even the food one raises or, more recently, the money one earns at a job is not his to keep if someone else in the family—especially the *matai*—needs it. The result is a kind of communalism, or "social security," which worked very well in the old days of a purely subsistence economy, particularly if the *matai* was a wise administrator. Now that money has become more important and some notion of property ownership has been introduced, the *matai* system is undergoing modifications since many of the younger people think it unfair. However, it still remains the heart of Samoan life.

One result of this family concept is that a young Samoan often will not live with his parents, but will decide to move in with some other relative, who is obliged to take him in.

Samoan life includes a good deal of ceremony and observation of tradition. One of the most important rituals is the drinking of 'ava, or *kava*, a sacred ceremony which accompanies such social events as chiefs' meetings, feasts, celebrations, and mourning. *Kava*, prepared from the root of a pepper plant and water, is not alcoholic, but if taken in large quantities, it has a somewhat paralyzing effect on the legs. It is served in coconut-shell cups, from a large, round, often many-legged, carved wooden bowl, and the preparation and serving follow a rigid traditional pattern.

America got the best harbor when Samoa was divided, but very little land came with it: Tutuila is only about eighteen and one half miles long and seven miles wide. Most of the island except the southwest end is quite mountainous. Although the Samoans plant coconuts, bananas, taro, and a few other crops, often on extremely steep slopes, for the consumption of Tutuila's 25,000 residents, no large-scale agriculture is possible.

American Samoa produces a small amount of copra for export, but for most of the century government jobs have been the most important source of cash income. Until 1951, the Navy base was Samoa's leading industry, and its closing left a serious economic gap. In recent years, two tuna canneries on the north side of Pago Pago Bay have given a tremendous boost to the economy. It was hoped that Samoans would work on the tuna vessels, since Polynesians originally were great sailors, but such has not been the case. The Samoans don't like the hard life of weeks or months at sea away from their homes. It is reported that some of them get seasick. So the fishing boats today are manned by three thousand or more Asian citizens—Koreans, Nationalist Chinese, and Japanese—while the canneries employ Samoan men and women to process the frozen fish brought in by the boats.

Wages paid to Samoans, either in government employment or in private industry, are low—an important reason for the commercial success of the cannery. The typical Samoan working full-time for pay probably earns less than two thousand dollars a year. While this may be enough for him to live comfortably Samoan style—particularly with various members of his *aiga* contributing not only cash but food—it does not permit luxuries. And he's dissatisfied when he hears of salaries earned by non-Samoans who come to the islands to work and of the wages generally paid in the States. As is true in many other parts of the Pacific, the pay given an outsider—government official, business executive, teacher, clerk, skilled mechanic, construction worker, or technician—is probably three to five times the salary paid a local person doing the same work. The practical reason for this is clear: an outsider wants the same pay he would get where he came from plus some additional incentive pay, and he doesn't intend to live in the native style. In August, 1969, the new governor, John M. Haydon, announced plans to abolish the double-pay standard for government workers.

Thousands of hopeful American Samoans have moved to Hawaii or the U. S. West Coast to try to earn higher wages, perhaps to come back rich and live the rest of their days in Samoa. But many of these Samoans, both by training and from their relatively poor command of English, have been able to find only low-paying jobs, and their new higher living expenses rapidly devour their pay. A Samoan chief overseas often finds himself a ghetto dweller, respected only by his resident relatives.

In an attempt to improve the future of both the American Samoans in Samoa and those who wish to try life elsewhere, the administration has recently concentrated its effort on education. Until 1946 there was no public high school; now there are several. While Samoan is the language used in the home, the public schooling is bilingual, both Samoan and English. Here a problem arose, for the majority of the teachers were Samoans who often were not proficient in English. The solution to the problem was to introduce instruction by television, thereby teaching the children and strengthening the ability of the teachers at the same time.

Since 1964, educational television has been not just an accessory to the educational program; it has been an important part of it. From the top of 1,600-foot Mount Alava, beside Pago Pago Bay, a transmitter sends out school programs at various grade levels over six different channels. Each student usually gets at least an hour a day of televised programs at school, and in the evenings the families watch not only educational programs but also reruns of old American commercial television series.

When the transmitter was installed, an aerial tramway was constructed on cables nearly a mile long, extending from the mountaintop clear across Pago Pago Bay to a low hill on the town side. This tramway, formerly used to hoist materials to the construction site, is now used daily by transmitter technicians to get to their jobs, and also by some high-school students from the far side of the island to commute to the school in town, though they have to climb the mountain every morning. The tramway has also become a tourist attraction; for two dollars and fifty cents (students and workers don't pay this much) one can ride up to the station for an unexcelled view of the island, the bay, and on a good day, a view across the channel to Western Samoa.

The large, muscular Samoans are great athletes and love sports. (Some have succeeded in professional football, baseball, and boxing in the United States.) Pago Pago Bay is the site of one of their favorite intervillage competitions, boat racing. The longboats used for racing, are about one hundred feet long. They are built locally of planked construction and hold three or four dozen men. You can hear a longboat coming a mile down the bay, the coxwain beating a loud rhythm on a five-gallon drum.

The arrival of a passenger liner in American Samoa is a big event. At the dock, music and dancing welcome the visitors. In town the policemen, who on ordinary days wear pants, on boat day put on their more formal and picturesque red-and-black *lava-lava*s, or wraparound skirts. Samoan women bring their handicrafts—woven bags and mats, wood carvings, *tapa*, objects made of turtle or sea shells—to a large market across the street from the town's open square. A newly-developed "village" nearby offers the tourists an opportunity to buy handicrafts and

A Samoan racing longboat rests near Pago Pago Harbor.

see them made and to take photographs. When the ship leaves, there is another program of music and dancing at the dock, featuring a group of older women dressed in floral prints who unroll their mats and perform graceful dances sitting cross-legged. As the ship leaves, the tramway car moves out over the channel, dropping basketfuls of flowers on the departing vessel.

Sunday is another important day in Samoa. The Samoans put on their best clothes—*lava-lava*, shirt, tie, and usually a jacket for men, and long light-colored dresses for women. Enthusiastic churchgoers, they often attend more than one service each Sunday at the many churches on the island.

A local truck-bus with wooden benches provides an interesting ride to the village of Tula, about fifteen miles away at the north end of Tutuila. Tula, though small, has a good district school and a rather modern look at its center, where hurricane-destroyed *fale*s were replaced by rectangular houses. The road from town leads around the head of Pago Pago Bay, through the small Pago Pago village itself, past the tuna canneries, then on through five or six more villages and a number of small clusters of *fale*s. In the country it appears that a Samoan male over the age of ten hardly feels fully dressed unless he's carrying a large keen machete, which gives him a warlike appearance. Actually, the machete is an all-purpose implement for clearing weeds and brush, harvesting bananas, opening coconuts, or just whacking for pleasure. On this ride, one notes a characteristic feature of the Samoan coastline near each group of houses, a little pier, on the end of which perches the community outhouse—necessary because, except in the Pago Pago area, American Samoa has no sewage system.

For a slower and closer look at Samoa, one may walk across the island on a road that leads over a pass through the mountains behind Pago Pago Bay to the attractive village of Fagasá. A stream with *fales* beside it follows the steep valley down to Fagasá. Samoans love to have running water for their laundry, which typically is done by scrubbing the clothes on a flat rock, often beating them with a stick. Soap is used if it is available. Samoans also use streams for their frequent baths, but more often they bathe under a running faucet, which may be five feet or more above the ground. Each village or group of houses has such a faucet, which may or may not be surrounded by a bathhouse. Except for small children, a public bath is taken while the bather is at least partially clothed, cleansing both bather and clothing at the same time.

Fagasá looks more like a Samoan village than does most of the area around Pago Pago Bay. Either it suffered less loss from the hurricane than other parts of the island or the residents repaired the damage without government aid, for there are fewer hurricane-relief houses. A number of other villages along the north coast of Tutuila lack roads and can be visited only by steep trails over the mountain or by the government supply boat which calls several times a month.

Government ships also visit the three small high islands of the Manu'a group, seventy miles east of Tutuila, where about three thousand American Samoans live in a less westernized manner than the Tutuilans, although they, too, receive educational television. Swain's Island, a small, coconut-producing atoll with a population of about one hundred, lying two hundred miles north of Samoa, but not geologically part of the Samoan group, has been administered as part of American Samoa since 1925. Rose Atoll, eighty miles east of the Manu'a group, is uninhabited.

Western Samoa

Apia, the capital of Western Samoa, is less than eighty miles from Pago Pago, on the 430-square-mile island of Upolu. The channel between the two Samoas is only about fifty miles wide, but the easiest way to cross it is aboard one of the DC-3's operated by Polynesian Airlines, the pride of the independent state of Western Samoa.

Western Samoa became a German colony in 1899, after Germany had exerted economic influence in the islands since 1856. The Germans realized how well adapted the big islands of Samoa were to large-scale agriculture, and they introduced a plantation system, concentrating at first on coconuts and cotton. Cattle were used to keep down the weeds in coconut groves. Cotton, which had originally been profitable as a result of the American Civil War, eventually faded from the picture, and cocoa and rubber were introduced. Finding that the Samoans were not attracted to plantation work, the Germans imported contract laborers from Micronesia, Melanesia, and a few Polynesian islands in the early years; after 1900 most such labor came from either Melanesia or China. Agricultural research and experimentation sought new crops and improved production methods.

Under the influence of German efficiency, Samoa might have continued to grow economically, though possibly the major benefits would have been to the German empire, not to the Samoan people, who had already given up control over large areas of their islands. It must be admitted, however, that the Germans were able to clarify the land situation; previously, foreign land claims (obviously overlapping) had amounted to more than twice the whole area of German Samoa! But World War I came, Germany lost her empire, and New Zealand military forces occupied Western Samoa in 1914. After 1920, New Zealand continued to administer Western Samoa under a League of Nations mandate. For some years, the great lack of understanding between the administrators and the Samoans resulted in unrest, a lack of cooperation, and even bloodshed. Economic and social changes which New Zealand thought desirable proved unpopular. "Samoa for the Samoans" became a nationalistic slogan, and a group called the Mau actively worked against the New Zealanders. The rubber plantations failed through no fault of the administration, and other plantation agriculture suffered from the world-wide depression of the late 1920's and early 1930's.

A new era in Samoa began when New Zealand itself had a change of government in 1936. A gradual reconciliation came about between Samoa and her governors, and steps were taken toward Samoan self-government. After World War II, New Zealand's mandate became a United Nations trusteeship. Finally, a constitution was drawn up. A plebiscite in 1961 showed that the Samoans desired independence, and on January 1, 1962, Western Samoa became an independent nation. In 1970 the cabinet unanimously voted to join the British Commonwealth.

Strong ties with New Zealand remain, however. There is still a New Zealand high commissioner for Western Samoa, but he is now a consul, not an administrator of the country. New Zealand has continued to offer financial aid and technical assistance to the young state in education, in the development of Polynesian Airlines, and in other programs. New Zealand also serves as Western Samoa's diplomatic representative in international affairs. Many Western Samoans go to New Zealand for higher education or to work. United Nations agencies have helped in economic development, and the United States has sent several hundred Peace Corps volunteers to work in community development, health, and education.

The government of Western Samoa, while embodying certain democratic principles, continues to place power and importance in the *matai*. The Legislative Assembly consists of forty-five Samoan members elected by the eight thousand or more *matai* and two European members elected by the citizens of non-Samoan ancestry. Four important Samoan families are considered of royal rank, and the custom has been established that the head of state be chosen from one of these four families. The Prime Minister, appointed by the Head of State, has come from another such family.

On a map Western Samoa looks like two big fish facing one another, fighting over the possession of two small islands between them. The westernmost fish, Savai'i (660 square miles), is a sort of flatfish; the easternmost, Upolu (430 square miles), is more like a cod. Both have rather poorly defined tails.

Upolu is about forty-seven miles long. Since the airfield is near the western end, the plane from Tutuila flies along most of the length of the island. A mountainous ridge up to 3,600 feet high extends down the center. The north coast has several large

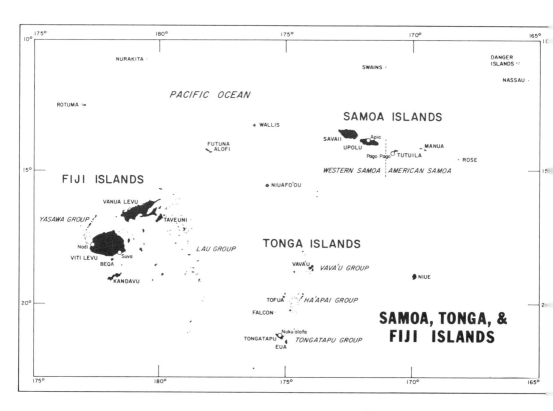

bays in its eastern half; in the west, a barrier reef lies a mile or two out from shore beyond a lagoon. Apia, about one-third the way from the west end, lies around a semicircular bay behind an opening in the reef. Faleolo Airport, still entirely grass-covered in 1970, is about twenty miles beyond. Savai'i lies about ten miles away across a channel.

Besides a few businessmen, officials, and tourists, the plane's passengers typically include American Samoans coming to call on their cousins in Western Samoa and Western Samoans re- turning from a visit to Tutuila. The small, rambling wooden terminal is crowded with friends and relatives to welcome them and to say *tofa* (good-bye) to those leaving on the return flight. A rattling bus provides transportation along the twenty miles of road to Apia.

Western Samoa is less westernized in outward appearance than American Samoa. Since the Western Samoan finds it hard to pay for lumber, glass, and galvanized metal, he is more apt to continue building his thatched-roofed *fale.* The traditional costume is more in evidence, with men wearing *lava-lava*s rather than pants.

The dozens of villages on the way to Apia present a panorama of Samoan life and its interests. Each village has its church (or two or three), usually of quite imposing construction. Metho- dists, Congregationalists, Roman Catholics, Mormons, Seventh Day Adventists, and other denominations are represented. It also has its meetinghouse where the chiefs gather and, not far from the water, usually a shed to house the longboat used in intervillage competition. Each village green has a cricket pitch, for the game of cricket is practically a national sport, though a Britisher would hardly recognize the game. Instead of eleven on a team, Samoan cricket is more of a community activity, with fifty to a hundred men, women, and children on each side. Children practice the game, using the stem of a coconut frond for a bat and a ball of locally grown rubber.

Children walking to their schools wave as the bus passes. Women are heading to and from the communal water spigot. Some are washing their clothes there while others chat as they

A group of Samoan children happily pose at Apia, Western Samoa.

patiently await their turn. The walls of the *fale*s are all rolled up. Inside, women are sweeping with palm-rib brooms or sitting on the floor, sewing or weaving mats.

Some of the men, machetes in hand, are heading for the coconut groves or the family plot to gather food for the day. Others are out toward the reef in outrigger canoes, fishing or perhaps pulling in nets that had been set the night before. Still other men are lying on their mats at home, resting and thinking over their breakfasts. Work in Polynesia does not follow a clock; it is done when necessary and convenient.

Apia is a picturesque South Sea port city of about 26,000— over a quarter of the island's population. Behind it rises the green peak of Mount Vaea. The main waterfront street has only European-style buildings—trading companies, shops, agencies, and churches—but one needs to go only a few blocks from the waterfront to find families living in typical *fale*s, some of which may have electrical appliances. It is surprising to look into a sideless *fale* and see a bare-topped Samoan wearing his *lava-lava* talking on a telephone.

The island of Upolu was the home of Robert Louis Stevenson during the last four years of his life. In search of a climate that would help his tuberculosis, Stevenson traveled to various parts of Europe and America. In June, 1888, he, his wife, and stepson left San Francisco aboard a chartered yacht for the Marquesas, the Tuamotus, Tahiti, and Hawaii, where he stayed six months. A trading schooner then took the Stevensons to the Gilbert Islands and Samoa. Here Stevenson bought three hundred acres of property at Vailima ("five streams"), in a broad valley behind Apia to build a house and establish a plantation. His home was staffed by Samoan servants, and Stevenson soon earned great affection and respect from Samoans, commoner and chief alike.

His plantation did not really become productive, but his pen was, and he continued to write until his death from a stroke in December, 1894. Besides writing several nonfiction accounts of the South Seas, Stevenson wrote two South Sea novels (*The Wrecker* and *The Ebb-Tide*) in collaboration with his stepson, Lloyd Osbourne, and a collection of stories, *Island Nights' Entertainments*, which includes "The Beach of Falesá," a fine tale set in Samoa.

Stevenson's house at Vailima lies at the end of a tree-bordered drive. The Samoans—including chiefs, who usually do not engage in manual labor—constructed a road for Stevenson during the last year of his life, and at the entrance to the drive stands

The historical residence of Robert Louis Stevenson at Vailima brings back memories of good reading.

a monument on which a bronze plaque reads, in both English and Samoan:

THIS IS THE ROAD OF LOVING HEARTS
HEWN BY THE PEOPLE OF SAMOA FOR TUSITALA—
ROBERT LOUIS STEVENSON—WHOSE RESTING PLACE
LIES ON MOUNT VAEA ABOVE

Stevenson's rambling two-story house, which underwent extensive repairs following the hurricane of 1966, is now the official residence of the Head of State of Western Samoa. It is open to visitors for only a few hours during the week. After crossing Vailima's main stream, one can take the steep trail up which Stevenson's Samoan friends bore his frail body.

In a clearing at the top, with a magnificent view of the valley, the ocean, and Stevenson's own house far below, is Stevenson's tomb. On one end is a plaque to Stevenson's wife, Fanny, who survived him by twenty years and whose ashes were brought back from California to be buried in her husband's grave. One side of the tomb bears a plaque to "Tusitala" ("Teller of Tales") with the biblical speech of Ruth to Naomi. On the other side, a plaque bears Stevenson's name and dates and his own epitaph, "Requiem":

Under the wide and starry sky,
Dig the grave and let me lie.
Glad did I live and gladly die,
And I laid me down with a will.

This be the verse you grave for me:
Here he lies where he longed to be;
Home is the sailor, home from the sea,
And the hunter home from the hill.

The road along the north side of Upolu, east of Apia, like the road from the airport, passes through a number of typical villages. There is a variety of coastline: rocky points, black-sand beaches and white-sand beaches, and in some places a lagoon inside a reef.

Twenty miles from Apia, near the village at the head of a bay, is Falefá Falls, where the river tumbles seventy-five to one hundred feet over a cliff. Upstream, only a few hundred feet from the falls, children swim unconcernedly in the river. From here, the road climbs up wide Falefá Valley over a pass to the south side of the island.

Along the unpaved main road, bridges look down on pools in which women wash dishes and kitchenware or chat and do the laundry while children play in the water.

Farther around the island is the village of Lefanga, where *Return to Paradise*, with Gary Cooper, was filmed in the 1950's. If ever a spot looked like an ideal South Sea village, this one does —clusters of conically roofed *fales* and tall coconut trees behind a wide, curving beach of white sand. And the only people in sight are Samoans.

Passing from cluster to cluster of *fales* in the outskirts of Apia (a cluster representing the members of a single family), a visitor meets friendly Samoan greetings and questions. At a minimum, a Samoan will say "Hello" as you approach him and "Good-bye" as you pass him. More often, the youngsters want to chat a little, and their typical questions are "Where are you going?" "What is your name?" "When did you come to Samoa?" "Where do you live?" "When do you go?" followed by the concluding "Thank you" and "Good-bye." We in turn use our two words of Samoan, *"Talofa"* (hello) and *"Tofa"* (good-bye). Although gardens surround the *fales*, many of the families living here—and in the smaller coastal villages as well—have additional plots some distance, often miles, inland. Samoans spend a good deal of time walking to work on these plots.

On a point just west of Apia Harbor, at Mulinu'u, are the observatory, established by the Germans in 1902; the burial ground of Samoan royalty; the Independence Monument, a green where important ceremonies are held; and the Legislative Assembly building—a huge domed building with architecture derived from the traditional Samoan style.

And what is the future of the Samoan way as we draw toward

the last quarter of the twentieth century? Samoa's two main problems are its alarming rate of population growth and its rather static economy, supported by copra, cocoa, and bananas. Additional economic development—whether through large-scale agriculture, tourism, or industry—will inevitably mean introducing a number of ways that are not the Samoan way, that might threaten the family organization and a family's communal ownership of land. Over two-thirds of the land in Western Samoa is "customary land," owned by family groups, and cannot be bought or sold, though it may be leased.

In the first few years of Western Samoa's independence, the government was opposed to tourist development. On second thought, however, government opinion changed, and now tourism is viewed as an activity which can make up the deficit between the country's imports and exports. Resort hotels in rural areas are planned, as well as expansion of the facilities in Apia.

Besides tourism—on a limited basis—a few other areas are being investigated for economic development. Looking at the success of American Samoa's canneries, Western Samoa is investigating fishery development, with perhaps Japanese and Korean assistance. Such a project would not run into the complex problem of land rights!

From Samoa's land resources, cattle and timber production are mentioned as possibilities, although the native forest reserves could be easily depleted and systematic commercial cropping of either native or introduced trees on tree farms would take some years to establish. The island of Savai'i, with 660 square miles to Upolu's 430 and a population only forty percent as large as Upolu's, offers space for agricultural expansion, although much of the soil is poor. Some of the land is covered with lava flows from as recently as 1911. Savai'i can be reached by small ferries operating from the western end of Upolu, and has a tiny airfield. In the late 1960's, a wharf was built, and a deep-water harbor was created by blasting and dredging through the reef to give this island's exports direct access to large vessels.

Western Samoa's educational system, still rather closely modeled on New Zealand's, has primary and intermediate schools, in which the English language is used increasingly as the student advances. At the age of fifteen or sixteen, many students go on to the secondary schools for several years, and thence perhaps to a "college" (equivalent to an American high school), or an institute which will prepare them for a trade, or for agriculture, teaching, or admission to institutions of higher education over-

Policeman directs traffic at an intersection in Apia.

seas. Various mission schools supplement the public education program.

Health is a constant problem in both Samoas. For years, the major diseases have included leprosy, tuberculosis, yaws, worms, and filariasis. Yaws is a disease which causes great open sores in its early stages. Filariasis, caused by a blood-stream parasite, can result in a grotesque deformity called elephantiasis. For all of these diseases or parasites, modern drugs or vaccines are quite effective; yaws has been eliminated from American Samoa already. But these diseases need to be guarded against constantly and drugs brought to the people. In Western Samoa, Department of Health officers, Peace Corpsmen, and representatives of the World Health Organization work constantly on health, sanitation, and dental problems.

The per capita income of Western Samoa's residents (nearly 150,000) is no more than a third of that in American Samoa. Are the Western Samoans less happy, then? It may be a romantic oversimplification for a visitor to say that the Western Samoans seem happier.

The American Samoans would probably not—if they were given the choice—like at this time to give up their advantages to join Western Samoa. Western Samoa voluntarily and proudly chose independence and a more traditionally Samoan way of life, poor though it may be in material things. This may only have slowed down the introduction of alien values. But in the past, the Samoan way has been remarkably resilient—to missionaries, the Germans, and the New Zealanders. What was not liked was rejected; what was accepted was somehow remodeled to make it fit the Samoan pattern. The longer this attitude continues, the longer the proud Samoans will continue to retain their individuality, as the largest group of people to keep a distinctively Polynesian identity.

Tonga,
the Friendly Kingdom

The flight of about five hundred miles across the Pacific from Samoa to Tonga is a journey from the newest independent Polynesian state to the oldest independent Polynesian kingdom. It is also a flight into tomorrow, for Tonga is just on the western side of the International Date Line. This imaginary line passes through the Pacific in a north-south direction at a longitude of 180°, or halfway around the world from London. It arbitrarily marks where a new day begins, so that people the world over can keep the date straight, just the way the starting line on a circular race track marks where a new lap begins. The Date Line doesn't follow the 180° mark exactly; in the South Pacific it bends 500 miles to the east so that all the Fiji and Tonga islands will be together and both will keep time with New Zealand.

Archeologists are still trying to determine when Tonga was first settled by Polynesians. Radioactive-carbon dating of a Tongan specimen has yielded a fifth-century B.C. date, the earliest in all Polynesia. If, as is generally believed, the Polynesians came from the west, they must have been living in some of the islands between Tonga and Asia—Fiji perhaps—even earlier. It is also interesting that thousands of fragments of prehistoric pottery have been found in Tonga. Unless pottery was brought in by interisland trade, this evidence indicates that the art of pottery making was lost by the Tongans; it was never introduced into most of Polynesia and has not been practiced in Tonga in historic times.

Of the prehistory of Tonga, little has come down to us except mute archeological fragments. The genealogies of the ruling family date back to perhaps A.D. 950, when the first Tu'i Tonga assumed both political and religious leadership in the islands. (*Tu'i* is a title which signifies this position.) Twenty-four generations later the Tu'i Tonga of that period decided to keep only the religious functions and turned the duties of ruling over to his brother, who took the title of Tu'i Ha'atakalaua. After six generations, the new ruling dynasty again split with the result that for several centuries there were three titled royal lines.

The late Queen Salote, who inherited the throne from her father, had two of the royal lines in her blood. Her husband, the prime minister, was heir to the third of the royal lines, so the present King Taufa'ahau Tupou IV (Salote's son) and his brother Prince Tu'ipelehake, the premier, reunited in their blood all three of the royal dynasties. They are the forty-fourth generation in a direct line tracing back to the first Tu'i Tonga.

A Tu'i of Tonga was not always able to maintain undisputed rule over his widespread fleet of islands. Frequently a strong chief, perhaps a relative of the king, would assume control over an island or group of islands, and rivalries between leaders were common.

During many periods the Tongans engaged in both trade and war with the Fijians to the west. Indeed, the Lau Islands, a Fijian group lying between Fiji's major islands and Tonga, are inhabited today by people largely of Tongan ancestry. Even as late as the middle 1800's, Tongan chiefs from the Lau Islands were greatly concerned with Fijian affairs.

Tonga consists of from one hundred and fifty to two hundred islands in three main groups: Vava'u, Ha'apai, and Tongatapu. Some of them are mere dots of coral; others are high volcanic islands, and some are a combination of lava rock and coral limestone.

Because of the distance between islands, not all of Tonga was discovered at the same time or by the same European navigator. The Dutch seamen Schouten and Le Maire approached two of the remote northern islands in 1616. In 1643 Abel Tasman, sailing into the Pacific from the East Indies, discovered some of the southern Tongas and gave them good Dutch names (which didn't stick), such as Amsterdam and Rotterdam. More than a century elapsed before the next European, Captain Samuel Wallis, fresh from his discovery of Tahiti, paused for a day at one of the northern islands.

The great Captain Cook was the first Westerner to become a real enthusiast of Tonga. On his second Pacific voyage, he visited the southern islands of Tongatapu in the fall of 1773, and the next year called at the Ha'apai group. He liked the islands so much that on his third voyage, three years later, he spent over two months in the Ha'apai and Tongatapu Islands. So well was Cook entertained on his stays in Tonga that he applied the name "Friendly Islands," a term which has been affectionately used ever since.

A dozen years later, following the mutiny on the *Bounty*, Captain William Bligh put in at the island of Tofua. He hoped to get additional food and water for his twenty-three-foot open boat, already heavily loaded with nineteen passengers and a limited stock of provisions. He found the Tongans not so friendly. They harassed the poorly armed Englishmen and eventually attacked, killing Bligh's quartermaster before the boat could put out to sea. Amazingly, his was the only death among Bligh's men before the frail craft arrived at Timor, 3,600 miles away, a month and a half later.

Another early visitor to Tonga was the almost legendary Will Mariner, who left London in 1804, at the age of thirteen, as captain's clerk aboard the British whaler and privateer *Port-au-Prince*. Following the death of its captain at sea, the ship was poorly commanded at the time she put in at an island which the powerful chief Finau II controlled. A carefully planned attack resulted in the capture of the ship and the massacre of most of those aboard. The ship was burned for the nails and other metal she contained. A few members of the ship were spared, however, including the fifteen-year-old Mariner, who was taken under Finau's protection and treated like a chief's son. His account of four years in Tonga, written with the aid of a London doctor, John Martin, is one of the classics of early Pacific literature.

Mariner finally left Tonga aboard a visiting British ship and never returned. His narrative relates that when Captain Cook visited the islands in 1777 Finau I had plotted to kill Cook and seize his ships. Cook left before the plot could be carried out, without even being aware of his narrow escape!

Like most of the Pacific islands, Tonga was the scene of intensive missionary efforts. The London Missionary Society withdrew in 1800 after several years of unsuccessful work, but in 1828 the Methodist Church established a mission, and Tonga today is predominately Methodist. The man who became King Tupou I was baptized in 1831 as George. The first king of

Calling the congregation to church in Tonga, the bell fills a real need.

modern Tonga, he ruled for more than forty-seven years, until his death in 1893, a reign exceeded in length only by that of his granddaughter Salote ("Charlotte"). Roman Catholicism was also early established in Tonga; later the Church of England came. Other missions, including that of the Mormons, are active today.

Great Britain kept a watchful eye on Tonga. The introduction of Methodism as the foremost religion gave Britain a priority among European nations, and a British consul to Tonga was appointed as early as 1857. The French also had a slight interest due to their Catholic missions, and the Reverend Shirley Baker (a Methodist missionary who became prime minister) had granted certain rights to the Germans. Late in 1899, when Germany took control of Western Samoa, she yielded her rights in Tonga, and Britain assumed protection of the Tongan kingdom.

Under British protection, Tonga remained an independent kingdom, not a colony, and is the only inhabited island in Polynesia, Micronesia, and Melanesia which has never been completely under foreign control. The British protectorate officially ended in June 1970, although Britain continues financial aid and is willing to help Tonga in case of internal disorders or external problems. Tonga's constitution, adopted in 1875, provides for a Legislative Assembly consisting of seven cabinet ministers, seven nobles, and seven elected representatives.

One of the more interesting Tongan islands, Niuafo'ou, stands by itself, to the northwest. It is shaped like a huge doughnut, over five miles across and 850 feet high, with a three-mile lake occupying its central crater. Three or four destructive eruptions in this century added to the bulk of the island but destroyed fertile agricultural land. On several occasions, the government has evacuated most of the inhabitants, but many of the homesick islanders have returned to tend their coconut plantations and to replant their bananas and yams.

Since Niuafo'ou has no harbor, ships cannot use it as a port. In years past, when steamers came near the island, outgoing mail was entrusted to a strong swimmer, who would carry the mail out in a tin can wrapped in greased paper and receive a similar can of incoming mail. This practice gave the island its nickname, "Tin Can Island." Today an outrigger canoe, powered by an outboard motor, is used for the "Tin Can" mail, much of which is destined for stamp collectors all over the world.

About two hundred and fifty miles from Samoa lies the Vava'u group, whose main island, of uplifted coral limestone, is about ten miles long and has a peak nearly seven hundred feet above sea level. The widespread Ha'apai group is a hundred miles farther south. Most of these are low, coral islands, no more than fifteen feet above sea level, standing on a huge submarine reef formation. In the western Ha'apais are volcanic islands, one of which, Tofua, is, like Niuafo'ou, an almost perfectly circular crater containing a freshwater lake. It is no longer regularly inhabited because of occasional eruptions, although its black volcanic stones are gathered by Tongans for use in decorating graves. It was off Tofua, then inhabited, that the mutiny of the *Bounty* took place in 1789.

Also among the volcanic Ha'apai islands is one of the most unusual in the Pacific: Falcon Island, the "Jack-in-the-Box Island." It has been up and down several times within a century. In 1877 smoke was reported coming from the ocean in a spot where a shoal had been noted. In 1885 the island rose from the sea and eventually attained a height of nearly three hundred feet and a length of almost two miles. However, by 1898, wave action, and perhaps sinking, reduced it to a sea-level reef. In 1927 Falcon Island rose again in a series of violent eruptions, this time reaching a height of 475 feet and a length of over two miles. After about ten years, volcanic action ceased, and the island again began to vanish. A single coconut tree planted on it by a party of visitors survived for a few years, but disappeared with the island in the early 1940's.

The southernmost group is named after its main island, Tongatapu. Approaching from the north, a plane first flies over a dozen small islets, with attractive beaches here and there, and numerous reefs of varying size and extent, some enclosing shallow lagoons. Between them are deeper channels, revealed by their darker water. The patterns of the islets and reefs are fascinating, as are the colors: dark blue, light blue, aquamarine, green, and beige, with the white of the wave crests and surf.

Without any distinctive hills, Tongatapu reaches only 270 feet above sea level. In general triangular, measuring about eighteen miles from east to west and eight miles from north to south, Tongatapu is in size alone the most important island in Tonga. And it contains the capital city, Nuku'alofa, whose two piers project across a fringing reef to a deep-water channel, capable of being used by the biggest liners in the Pacific. The larger pier, the million-dollar Queen Salote Memorial Wharf, which was dedicated by King Taufa'ahau Tupou IV in 1967, is the largest single construction project ever completed in Tonga.

Nuku'alofa, a town of about twenty thousand, consists of single dwellings and small buildings laid out in regular blocks. Near the wharves, facing the waterfront, is a large structure of which the Tongans are extremely proud, the three-story Dateline Hotel, opened in 1966. East of the town lies the entrance to a large two-branched lagoon, one arm of which curves behind the town.

The small air terminal beside the grass runway proudly flies the red-and-white Tongan flag. Behind a fence made of airstrip matting stand the welcomers, mostly smiling Tongans, waving and shouting to their friends and relatives returning from far places. Some of the Tongans are dressed in informal western style, the men wearing slacks and sport shirts, but others wear the Tongan *lava-lava*s. The typical women's apparel is quite conservative, revealing the missionary influence. But the most characteristic element of the Tongan costume is the ceremonial mat, or apron, made of woven grass or pandanus leaves, wrapped around the middle on top of the dress or shirt and *lava-lava.*

A mat may be only a half-dozen inches wide. For important occasions, or to show deep respect, the mats are especially large and heavy, extending two or more feet from top to bottom, and the older the better, even if ragged and tattered. In 1965 and 1966, during the period of mourning for Queen Salote, the mats were especially large and venerable. To a newcomer, the attire looks as if the missionaries had covered the Tongans with foreign cloth and then the Tongans decided to show their independence by putting a traditional costume on top of the new.

Along the fourteen miles between the airport and Nuku'alofa, the scenery is decidedly rural with numerous banana and coconut plantations. In some places, rows of bananas alternate with rows of coconut trees, and occasionally there are rows of taro between the coconuts and the bananas. Copra is Tonga's biggest agricultural export, bananas second.

The Tongan houses along the road show modern influences, but often look much like the old native dwellings, some of which still stand. The primitive house is small and generally rectangular, although the ends may be rounded. The roof is thatched, and the sides, of woven coconut fronds, tend to be permanent, unlike the sides of Samoan houses. Tongatapu is farther from the equator than Samoa and subject to cooler weather, especially in August—since the seasons are "turned around" in the Southern Hemisphere. Though the days are pleasantly warm, the temperature of tropic nights here may drop into the fifties,

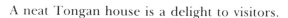

A neat Tongan house is a delight to visitors.

especially when a wind blows from the ice-coated Antarctic. For this reason, the modern Tongan house, while keeping the attractive shape and often the thatched roof of the old-fashioned houses, has sides made of boards.

Nearer Nuku'alofa are houses of purely Western design. Some even have a second story, and the more prosperous a picture window. A few are built of hollow tile, but wood predominates. The yards contain flowering or fruiting plants and trees—plumerias (frangipani), hibiscus, or bananas.

Many of the houses in town are surrounded by picket fences, and occasionally one sees an entrance gate over which is an arch of two huge pieces of bone—the jaws of a whale. These are trophies of Tonga's whaling days, now nearly over. There used to be a regular season, about September, when whales frequented the local waters and were hunted by the Tongans, principally for their flesh.

Tongan cemeteries also strike the visitor's eye. Each grave is surmounted by a mound of sand three to six or more feet high, so that a Tongan cemetery looks like a site where giants have been making sandpiles. Since piles of sand gradually disappear under wind and rain, faithful care and several techniques are used to preserve the graves: a covering of pieces of coral or stone may bank the sides, sometimes in patterns or with letters spelling out the name of the occupant. In some instances, walls protect the mounds; over a few graves small houses have been erected with roofs, sides, and even glassed windows.

The decorations placed over newly-made graves traditionally consist of fine pieces of *tapa* (bark cloth), woven mats, and strings of shells and other ornaments, usually hanging from a horizontal pole which rests on two uprights. In more recent years, fabrics such as rayon and silk have been used. Catholic cemeteries may contain more traditional tombstones bearing crosses, although they tend to topple in time.

Downtown Nuku'alofa reminds one of a small western or midwestern town of a generation ago. The shops, agencies, poolrooms, movie house, markets, government buildings, and a church or two are concentrated along a few blocks of a relatively wide road. Sidewalks are largely nonexistent except in front of some buildings with overhangs. Puddles from a sudden shower make progress hazardous for those with delicate shoes. The Tongans go barefoot or wear rubber sandals.

The modern method of transportation is the *ve'e tolu* taxi, which consists of a standard two-wheeled motorcycle pushing a large two-wheeled box with a bench around its edges. A passenger sits on the bench with his feet in the box. A roof keeps off the sun and rain. Some *ve'e tolu* hold only two passengers; in larger models, four or five are not really crowded. A natural hazard is that the driver, at the rear, has his view obstructed by his passengers.

Toward the lower end of the main street is a spacious, open, grassed area, where a market is held, especially on boat days. On the other side of the street, facing the exit from Tonga's older wharf, is a single-story, red-roofed, concrete building containing three important government agencies: the treasury, customs office, and post office. Tonga has long been a favorite with stamp collectors, and it frequently issues new stamps depicting local sights or commemorating historical events. One series featured stamps which had the shapes of various Tongan islands; another stamp was banana-shaped.

The Tongans are typically Polynesian, tall and brown—though there is considerable variation in the degree of brownness. One anthropologist states that as a group "Tongans are among the tallest of mankind." The men average well over 5 feet 8 inches, and this average means that a large number are 6-footers. There may be a greater degree of curliness or even kinkiness of hair because of centuries of contact with the somewhat different-appearing Fijians, who live less than five hundred miles to the west, but the difference between these and other Polynesians is hard for an outsider to detect. Their language would offer a better key to identifying Tongans for a person familiar with Polynesian dialects. All Tongans receive instruction in English at school, and although they prefer to converse in Tongan with one another, they are happy to speak English to visitors.

A *ve'e tolu* goes along the main street of Nuku'alofa.

Diagonally across the open square from the waterfront, inside a low-walled enclosure, are the Royal Chapel and the palace—white wooden buildings with red roofs. The Chapel has a steeple topped by a small cross. The Palace has two lower stories surrounded by verandas, some of which are enclosed, then rises to another story of gabled roofs. Above the front entrance a tower extends its cupola still another story into the air, and on top of that is a twenty-foot flagpole.

The palace is the official residence of His Majesty Taufa'ahau Tupou IV, King of Tonga and last recognized monarch of any of the island groups of Polynesia, ruler over nearly ninety thousand Tongans. And he is king-size, too: 6 feet 3 or 4 and 300 pounds.

On the other side of town is a large, open, grassy square, about a quarter of a mile on each side, in the center of which are

The Royal Palace at Nuku'alofa is home to the King of Tonga.

the tombs of all of the royal family who have died since the great George Tupou I in 1893. The most recent interment was that of the beloved Queen Salote, who ruled graciously, peacefully, and successfully from 1918 to 1965. She was modest but dignified and greatly beloved by her people. With her height of 6 feet 3 inches she had a truly regal stature. When she attended the coronation of Queen Elizabeth in London in 1953, she captured the hearts of the English people as she rode in the coronation procession in an open carriage, smiling, heedless of the cold rain.

Tongan dancing, which Captain Cook and other early voyagers described in detail, remains an important part of the culture and is always performed at festivities or other important occasions. In a mixed group, boys stand at one end of a line and girls at the other, using the same foot movements in a single dance, but moving their hands and arms somewhat differently.

Sunday in Tonga is even more strictly observed than in Samoa. Businesses are closed up tight; unnecessary travel, such as riding for pleasure, is frowned on, and sports are forbidden. The many churches are well-attended; passing any one of them, from the smallest to the largest, a Sunday stroller can hear—as in Samoa and Fiji—the congregation singing joyfully and skillfully in unforgettably resonant voices.

Tongan dancers perform at a Polynesian feast.

In several places in Tongatapu are mounds or artificial hills, up to one hundred feet or more in diameter, which rise as much as seven feet above the surrounding flat country. Some of these are house sites or ancient graves; others were built at chiefs' orders, as resting places where they might enjoy the view and the breezes. Another type of artificial mound, with a pit in the center of the top, was used by the chiefs in one of their favorite sports, pigeon snaring. Attracted by decoys, wild pigeons flew toward the mound, where men with a net strung between two poles trapped them and forced them down into the pit toward other men waiting to catch them.

There are also a few old native forts on the island, usually circular, with one or two walls and moats to aid in defense. The Tongans of old were skilled in the arts of war and frequently put these skills to use. In World War II, twenty-seven hundred Tongans volunteered to serve with the Allied forces. A number of them performed valiantly as commandos in fierce jungle fighting in the Solomon Islands.

The most impressive ancient graves on Tongatapu are the old royal tombs, or *langis*. Those along the road leading to the east end of the island are rectangular, in steps or tiers, like flattened pyramids. One of these structures is twelve feet high, in four steps, each of which is made of huge coral slabs. An archeologist determined that one of the slabs was 4.8 feet high, 23.8 feet long, and 1.3 feet thick! Royal genealogies and other oral history indicate that these *langis* were probably built between the eleventh and sixteenth centuries.

Even more striking than the royal tombs is Tonga's famous trilithon. The word *trilithon* means "three stones," and the structure is an archway consisting of two huge vertical stones with a third, horizontal stone set in notches at the tops of the two uprights. The opening, about 12½ feet square, faces due north and south. The crosspiece is 19 feet long, 4½ feet high, and 2 feet thick; the two uprights extend above the ground 15½ and 17 feet respectively and go down into the earth for an undetermined distance. Each upright measures about 14 feet by 4½ feet at its base.

This structure, whose Tongan name, *Ha'amonga-a-Maui*, means "the burden of Maui" (Maui was a powerful Polynesian god), was probably erected in the following manner: great slabs were cut from a soft coral-limestone cliff not far from where the trilithon stands; the large uprights were dragged up a temporary earthen incline and tipped into previously prepared holes, after which the crosspiece was dragged up the incline and set into the notches. Since the three stones weigh from thirty to forty tons each, the skill and manpower that this task required are truly impressive.

Was this arch erected for some ceremony or ritual, or even, as was once suggested, for use in a native game? Legendary accounts state that it was built by Tu'itatui, a Tongan king believed to have lived in the eleventh century. Each upright is said to symbolize—and even today bears the name of—one of Tu'itatui's sons, and the crossbar symbolizes the brotherly unity between the two.

The Ha'amonga-a-Maui trilithon has meanings lost in antiquity.

On the southwest side of Tongatapu is an interesting natural phenomenon, the Blowhole Coast. Here, for a half-dozen miles, wave action has created innumerable tunnels in a low coral-limestone cliff that drops down to deep water. Many of these tunnels end in small holes along the top of the cliff. When a wave or surge strikes the outer end of a tunnel, water rushes through it and shoots up in a saltwater geyser, sometimes more than fifty feet into the air. On a day when the tide and waves are right, one can watch hundreds of these blowholes in action.

Another kind of natural wonder is found in the village of Kolovai, near the west end of Tongatapu. In the middle of the village are four large casuarinas, or ironwood trees, in which live hundreds and hundreds of huge fruit bats, or "flying foxes." Whereas elsewhere on the island the bats are hunted, on these particular trees they are *tapu* (sacred), except to royalty. Flying foxes, which have rat-sized bodies and wingspreads up to three feet, are probably the only mammals that inhabited the Tongan Islands before the coming of the Polynesians.

Unfortunately, it is a few years too late to see another of Tonga's famous living wonders, the tortoise with the chiefly title

Flying foxes hang like strange fruit from a casuarina tree in Kolovai, Tongatapu.

Tu'i Malila, who is said to have been left behind as a present by Captain Cook. While generations of human beings lived and died, this tortoise roamed about the grounds of the palace in Nuku'alofa, treated with great respect. Although he became blind and suffered severe damage to his shell in several accidents, he lived until 1966, nearly one hundred and ninety years after Captain Cook was supposed to have left him.

Although one hates to spoil a good story, serious doubts have been cast on the origin of Tu'i Malila. He seems to have been the wrong species of tortoise for Captain Cook to have picked up en route to Tonga and so must have been left by some nameless sea captain who arrived later by a different route. The animal certainly lived for an extremely long time, however, and Tonga became so used to the idea of a chiefly tortoise that a new one was obtained from Madagascar a few months after the death of Tu'i Malila. Under the name of Tu'i Malila II, he fills the role of his predecessor.

The limestone structure of the islands has made possible the formation not only of the Blowhole Coast, but also of a number of caves. Two water caves in the Vava'u group have found a place in literature. One, in the small island of Hunga, is known as Will Mariner's Cave because Mariner's account of life in Tonga contains the cave's romantic story. A young chief was in love with a beautiful daughter of the head chief of Vava'u, but her father had promised her to another. It happened that the young chief had discovered the cave at Hunga, which can be entered only through an underwater opening. He persuaded her to elope with him and took her to the cave. She stayed there for some days; he visited her and brought food, meanwhile preparing their ultimate escape. Finally, he and his friends set out in a well-provisioned oceangoing canoe, stopped by the cave to pick up the girl, and sailed to safety in Fiji. The cave is still visited by good underwater swimmers, often with scuba equipment.

Another famous cave is Swallow's Cave, on the island of Vava'u itself. It too can be entered only from the sea, but since the entrance extends above the level of the ocean, one can enter it by boat to admire the unusually beautiful effects of light transmitted through and reflected from the water. This may be the cave, though he does not give its name, that Frank T. Bullen described in an exciting chapter of his whaling classic, *The Cruise of the Cachalot.* While exploring the cave in a whaleboat, Bullen and his boatmates found that a large bull whale had followed them inside. The harpooner almost instinctively thrust his weapon into the monster, and the boat survived a harrowing series of narrow escapes from being upset, crushed by the whale, or dashed against the rocks as the pain-crazed whale sought to escape. Meanwhile, the tide had risen so that the boat could not get out, and the men had to wait all night, while a horde of enormous sharks tore at the carcass of the whale, now and then crashing into the frail boat.

Present-day Tonga is faced with two major problems common to many Pacific islands. One is to find a basis for an economy at more than subsistence level; the other is an extremely high birthrate. Tongan copra and bananas have an export market, as do a few minor agricultural products, and native handicrafts produce a modest revenue. But this income will not pay for all the imported canned goods, flour, medical supplies, automobiles, motorcycles, cloth, and other manufactured goods that Tonga would like. Nor will it pay for a rapid improvement in education.

The King, who has a good education and is well traveled, is devoting considerable energy to finding ways to improve his country's economic position. Besides stepping up Tongan agricultural productivity, he has established a dried-coconut factory and the Tongan Shipping Line and has tried to encourage development of a fishing industry. Like other Pacific areas that have friendly people, a fine climate, and attractive scenery, Tonga ranks the tourist industry high in its future plans. Cruise ships have brought thousands of passengers annually to Nuku'alofa for a day or two. Now Tonga is building hotel and airport facilities on all three of its main groups to attract additional travelers.

In late 1968 oil was discovered in the Tongatapu group. Once its presence was announced, there was a great rush to see where oil might lie, and several Tongans were reported to have struck oil by merely using garden hoes! The exact extent and value of these oil deposits have not been determined, though a detailed survey by a group of large oil companies began in 1970. But a productive oil field of even limited size could have a large effect on Tonga's future if the resource is wisely handled so as to benefit the whole kingdom. Unplanned, carefree spending during a short boom could leave Tonga broke and disillusioned when the wells run dry. Incidentally, this discovery has raised hopes that perhaps other Pacific "continental" islands west of the Andesite Line may have previously unsuspected oil.

The rate of increase in the Tongan population is one of the highest in the Pacific. In 1920 the population was about 24,000; by 1939 it was 38,000. Since then it has more than doubled and would be even larger were it not for the fact that thousands of Tongans have gone to New Zealand or elsewhere in the Pacific to seek employment.

Ancient Tongan royal tomb lends a pensive mood to pastoral scene.

Each young male Tongan, upon reaching his majority at the age of sixteen, is entitled by law to use eight and a quarter acres of land—as long as he pays his taxes—upon which he may live and grow whatever he likes. At present no Tongan lacks the opportunity of making a subsistence living or even of making a small profit from his land. However, the plots still available are more remote and less desirable, and the total area of Tonga is not large. The land will one day run out if the population continues to increase. Among other measures, a birth-control clinic has been established.

In late 1967 and early 1968, 128 American Peace Corps volunteers came to Tonga to serve in the three main island groups and in some of the more remote islands, such as "Tin Can Island." Of the total, 60 were primary- and secondary-school teachers of science, mathematics, and English; 35 aided in nursing, sanitation, and other health projects; others were concerned with agriculture, cooperatives, tourism, marine biology, journalism, architecture, and secretarial training. It is hoped that the efforts of these workers will be of lasting benefit.

In his drive to maintain the spirit of Tonga while bringing it some of the best features of Western civilization, including improved medical and educational facilities, King Taufa'ahau Tupou IV appointed his brother, Prince Tu'ipelekahe, as his premier (a position that the King himself occupied while his mother ruled the kingdom). It has been pointed out that the two brothers make an admirable team—the King the more intellectual, though perhaps a bit aloof; the Premier a warmer person, closer to the people. One hopes that the two brothers, like the brothers symbolized in the massive uprights of the Ha'amonga-a-Maui trilithon, will carry successfully on their sturdy shoulders the future of their Friendly Kingdom.

Three Lonely Islands

EASTER ISLAND

Of the myriad islands in the South Pacific, three lonely islands deserve special mention—Easter, Pitcairn, and Norfolk.

Easter Island, at the far southeastern tip of the Polynesian triangle, lies 4,500 miles from New Zealand and 2,230 miles from the coast of South America. Known to its original inhabitants by its nearly forgotten Polynesian name, which means "The Navel of the World," it received its present name from the Dutch explorer Roggeveen, who discovered it on Easter Day, 1722.

Roughly triangular, it has a total area of less than fifty square miles and a length of about a dozen miles. At each corner is a large, extinct volcanic cone, the highest rising to nearly two thousand feet. The water supply is poor, with no large permanent streams, although two of the mountains have small lakes in their craters. Whatever trees the island may have had originally were probably small and few; by the time the Europeans arrived, trees were practically nonexistent. In recent years, trees from other parts of the Pacific have been planted in and near the inhabited areas.

When Captain Cook visited Easter Island, the population was estimated at nearly four thousand. In the nineteenth century, as a result of more frequent contact with the outside world, many Easter Islanders died from disease, moved away, or were kidnapped into slavery by Peruvian "blackbirding" expeditions. Of a thousand Easter Islanders taken by the Peruvians for labor, only fifteen survived to return, and some of these carried smallpox, which infected the other inhabitants. By the 1870's, the population was between one and two hundred, and the native culture was dead. Chile annexed the island in 1888. Today the population is over twelve hundred, mostly of mixed Easter Island and European blood. A sheep ranch is the sole industry.

But this small island has been the subject of numerous scientific investigations. The questions of when and how the Easter Islanders got to this lonely isle, who they were, and where they came from have been roundly debated. Thor Heyerdahl, the unconventional Norwegian anthropologist, believes they came from South America. The generally accepted theory, however, is that they came from the west or northwest, the first arrivals possibly coming from the Marquesas as early as the fourth century. The number of voyagers that found this Pacific outpost cannot be determined. The Easter language is a Polynesian dialect, but some of the prehistoric inhabitants or immigrants could have spoken other languages.

Let us assume that the Polynesians were the first to arrive, coming in large canoes from the west. They found a rather inhospitable home. If they brought dogs, pigs, and chickens, only the chickens survived. Certain plants—taro, yam, sweet potato, banana, sugarcane, and possibly a few others—came also. The immigrants may have found themselves cut off from the easy journey (with the prevailing winds) back westward because of the absence of large trees from which to make new seagoing canoes. Canoes usable for short fishing excursions were stitched together from small pieces of wood; even the paddles were made of several pieces. Bunches of reeds were used as rafts near shore.

The inhabitants developed their own form of Polynesian culture. They tattooed, and they worked not with wood, but in stone. They lived in caves or in structures largely made of stone. They built *ahu* (ceremonial platforms), reminiscent of those found in the Marquesas, for religious purposes, including burials. The most distinctive development, however, was that of the image *ahu*, which included gigantic stone statues, Easter Island's most amazing form of art.

The huge figures brood over this desolate island. Indeed, perhaps their expression, more than any other aspect of Easter's prehistory, has continued to reinforce the notion of Easter's "mystery." The heads, which have fully shaped fronts, but flat backs, show deep-browed eye cavities, long ears, sharply pointed noses, proudly pursed lips, jutting jaws, and a generally scornful air. The typical statue has a head, a neck, and a torso. Weighing tons, they range from images five feet high to a number in the twenty-foot range, and one is thirty-three feet tall. Originally, some bore separate cylindrical crowns or hats, extending several feet further upward. Some rest on broad bases; others have narrow bases buried in the ground. The source of

Giant stone images face seaward on lonely Easter Island.

these statues is no mystery, for the quarries, containing half-finished images, are on the inner slopes of one of Easter Island's craters.

Exactly why this art suddenly ceased is open to speculation. Perhaps war put an end to it, and the many toppled images may have been cast down by victors wishing to desecrate their rivals' shrines. At any rate, the gigantic sculptures were no longer being made at the time the first Europeans arrived. Over the years, a number of them were carried off to far parts of the world. Those remaining on the island are now a Chilean historical monument. With their imperturbable lofty stares they seem to be mocking time, collectors, and archeologists.

An Easter Island problem which may never be completely solved is that of the *rongorongo* boards, strips of wood on which columns of picture characters something like hieroglyphics were shallowly carved. Did these Polynesians have a written language? Unfortunately, the most learned Easter Islanders—the chiefs and priests—were wiped out during the island's depopulation, and nobody who could interpret the boards survived at the time they were first investigated in the 1860's. A number of specialists have worked on translations but with only partial success. Possibly the figures do not represent connected passages of language, but served priests only as memory aids in repeating long chants.

Today Easter Island is administered by the Chilean government through its navy. Because of the island's out-of-the-way location, ships rarely call, and those that do must anchor offshore. But since 1970, commercial jet planes have been able to stop at Easter on a schedule that will doubtless increase in frequency. Whereas few people would go thousands of miles out of their way to visit this fascinating but remote island, such a call has become more attractive as a stop on the route between Tahiti and Chile. Now adventurous travelers from North America may take a new circle-the-Pacific route, entering from the West Coast through Hawaii and ending up by flying from Easter to see some of South America before returning north.

PITCAIRN AND NORFOLK

Pitcairn Island, about 1,200 miles west of Easter and 350 miles southeast of Mangareva, is tinier and more formidable than Easter. It is less than two miles long and one mile wide. Largely surrounded by wave-pounded cliffs, it has no harbor—only one or two places where small boats can land in good weather.

Pitcairn is famous as the refuge of the mutineers from *H.M.S. Bounty.* Under Captain William Bligh, the *Bounty* came to Tahiti in late 1788. Bligh and his crew stayed for five months gathering breadfruit seedlings for transplantation in the Caribbean islands. Books and countless articles embodying fact, speculation, and fiction have been written and several popular movies have been made concerning the mutiny which occurred aboard the *Bounty* a few weeks after she sailed from Tahiti. Was the principal cause the tyranny of Bligh, a skilled officer who had sailed with Cook and who later held other responsible naval and military positions? Was it the lure of Tahiti, its soft climate and softer women? Did youthful rebelliousness and impetuosity put the mutineers in a situation which got out of control? In any event, under the leadership of twenty-four-year-old Fletcher Christian, master's mate, the mutiny took place in Tongan waters. Bligh and eighteen others, with no maps and only limited provisions, were placed in an overloaded open launch in which Bligh performed the miraculous feat of sailing 3,618 miles through the waters surrounding the Fijian islands, the Great Barrier Reef, and Torres Strait, to the island of Timor in the East Indies.

Since the British Navy would send out a search party sooner or later, the mutineers needed a refuge. The *Bounty* headed first for Tubuai, in the Austral Islands south of Tahiti, where an attempt to settle resulted in fighting. They returned to Tahiti to acquire hogs and other livestock. A second attempt at settling

on Tubuai was also a failure, and the *Bounty* again went back to
Tahiti, where a number of the crew chose to wait out their fate
in pleasant surroundings rather than risk the dangers of the sea
and unfriendly islanders elsewhere.

On her final departure from Tahiti under Christian, the *Bounty*
carried nine of her original crew, six Polynesian men, and a
dozen Polynesian women. For several months the fugitives
looked for a safe hideaway in the islands to the west, discovering
in the process the previously unknown large island of Rarotonga. Finally Christian decided to search for Pitcairn Island,
which he had read about in a book from the ship's library. It had
been sighted only once, over twenty years before, and was described as appearing uninhabited and difficult for landing. It
sounded like a good hideout.

The *Bounty* arrived in January of 1790. After deciding that the
island was suitable, the crew unloaded the ship, which was then
run aground and burned lest its presence give them away. Burial
sites, stone implements, images, platforms, and breadfruit trees
indicated that Pitcairn had previously been inhabited for a considerable length of time, doubtless by Polynesians.

From 1790 to 1808 the fate of the *Bounty* remained a mystery.
The survivors remaining on Tahiti were discovered, taken back
to England, and tried. Three of them were executed. Meanwhile, jealous rivalries between the Polynesians and the Englishmen on Pitcairn caused vicious, bloody battles, and in less than
ten years there remained only four Englishmen and ten women
from the original adult settlers. Within the next few years, two
of the remaining sailors met violent deaths; a third died perhaps
a natural death.

Eighteen years after the arrival of the *Bounty* at Pitcairn, the
American sailing vessel *Topaz*, under Captain Mayhew Folger,
called at the island. He found a colony of thirty-four women and
children and one former mutineer, John Adams, who had sailed
on the *Bounty* under the alias of Alexander Smith. Pitcairn had
by then become an extremely peaceful island with Adams leading his flock in religion and education to the best of his ability.
The colony's first additional immigrants, John Buffett and John

Evans, arrived in 1823. By 1825 the population had increased to sixty-six.

John Adams died in 1829, and the leadership of the island passed to George Hunn Nobbs, who had arrived the year before. Population growth and a drought threatened the people, and in 1831 all eighty-six of the people on the island moved to Tahiti with the help of British ships. Diseases caused the death of about one out of five, however, and within six months they went back to their old home.

Four thousand miles west of Pitcairn lies another of the Pacific's lonely islands, Norfolk, which was discovered, named, and claimed for England by Captain Cook on his second voyage. Although the thirteen-square-mile island was surrounded on nearly all sides by cliffs and had no harbor, Cook noticed the presence of an unusual variety of tall evergreen—the Norfolk Island pine—and native flax. These, he felt, could provide masts and sails for the ships of England.

In early 1788 Great Britain established the Colony of New South Wales in eastern Australia as a settlement for deported criminals, who could no longer be shipped to former North American colonies. Over a thousand convicts and their guards came to Sydney in the first fleet. Within a few weeks a ship was sent forth to establish a satellite colony on Norfolk Island to protect Britain's claim there and to raise food for the Sydney settlement.

The first Norfolk Island convict period lasted from 1788 to 1814. Although the population reached over a thousand, the island proved difficult to reach and hard to administer, and so it was abandoned. Even the promise of the pine trees and flax had not worked out: the trees were weakened by knots, and the flax was of poor quality.

Eleven years later, in 1825, a penal colony was reestablished on Norfolk, this time as a place for the most hardened criminals from New South Wales and from another convict settlement which had been established on the island of Tasmania. It was intended to be the "place of extremest punishment short of death," and it became just that. Hard labor, brutality of guards to prisoners, and incidents among the convicts themselves made the island a hell hole. Floggings were commonplace, and murders, mutinies, and executions stud the history of this period. Finally, humanitarian protest arose against Norfolk Island conditions, and once more it was decided to abandon the penal colony, moving most of the convicts to Tasmania. But another use for the island was planned.

After the unfortunate attempt to move to Tahiti in 1831, the Pitcairners had more than doubled in number by 1850. Droughts and consequent food shortages continued to threaten the island. Norfolk Island, with a quite similar climate, seemed an ideal relocation spot. Furthermore, the convict labor had built a number of excellently constructed stone and wooden buildings which the newcomers could use. In 1856 the entire Pitcairn population of 194 was moved to Norfolk, where a few

Kingston and the old convict ruins on Norfolk Island are guarded from the Pacific by a coral reef.

remaining prisoners and caretakers waited to turn the island over to its new residents.

Norfolk had a greater expanse of land and many advantages not possessed by Pitcairn; yet two years after the arrival on Norfolk, a pair of homesick families returned to Pitcairn; five years later four more families went back. Today their descendants form the population of Pitcairn.

Pitcairn's population slowly increased once more, reaching 233 by 1937. More recently, the population has steadily dropped as younger islanders have gone to New Zealand or elsewhere in search of a better life. In 1971 the population was 93, the majority older people. Even Pitcairn's lack of taxes is no attraction when there's no good way to earn money. Pitcairn has several times recovered from the status of an uninhabited island, toward which it again seems slowly headed.

On Norfolk Island, the larger number of *Bounty* people— bearing the "mutineer" names of Christian, Young, Adams, Quintal, and McCoy as well as the names of the Pitcairn immigrants, Buffet, Evans, and Nobbs—at first lived in the buildings left from the convict settlement at Kingston, then gradually spread over the island, on plots that were assigned to each family. Although the island was under the authority of New South Wales, they governed themselves for years, under a simple code, but in 1895 the first outside administrator was appointed. Today the island is a territory of Australia.

In 1866 the Melanesian Mission obtained government permission to occupy nearly one-eighth of Norfolk Island, somewhat to the dismay of the *Bounty* people, who had thought the entire island was theirs. Under an Anglican bishop, the Mission established a college to train native teachers from the islands of Melanesia, hundreds of miles to the north. In 1920 the Mission was moved to a site in Melanesia itself, in the Solomon Islands.

Norfolk's population grew, reaching a peak of over twelve hundred in the early 1930's. Of these, the majority were still descendants of Pitcairn Islanders, but other settlers, principally from Australia and New Zealand, had added to the number. During World War II the population dropped below eight hundred as Norfolk Islanders entered the armed forces or took war-related jobs overseas. Today, Norfolk has nearly fifteen hundred people and is still growing.

For sixty years, Norfolk was the site of an important station for the main Pacific telegraph cable from North America. The cable divided at Norfolk into two branches, one heading for New Zealand and the other for Australia. The cable was inactivated in 1962. The island's strategic position, halfway between New Caledonia and New Zealand, also made it a highly desirable site for a military airfield. Its construction, in 1942, destroyed one of the island's most cherished features, Pine Avenue, which extended straight for over a mile, with towering hundred-year-old pines at regular intervals along either side. The war-built airfield has become Norfolk's principal link with the outside world. Norfolk's steep cliffs rise from two to four hundred feet above the water; toward the center two "mountains," Mount Pitt and Mount Bates, reach one thousand feet. Just to the south are two uninhabited islands, low Nepean Island and barren Philip Island, an old volcano nearly as high as Norfolk.

At Kingston, where a cliffless low area stretches back from the water, are stone buildings and ruins remaining from the convict days. The high prison wall, topped with broken glass, has an imposing main gate and another "gallows gate," where hangings took place. The guards' old barracks are also surrounded by high walls—they could serve as forts in case of a prisoner uprising. During one twelve-month period 109 convicts "were shot by the sentries in self-defense and 62 were bayoneted to death."

The officers' bath and ruins of a crank mill, a lime kiln, a salt house, and other buildings remain. Government House, the home of Norfolk Island commandants in convict days, and of administrators in this century, stands on a rise, aloof from the other Kingston buildings. On the edge of the town is the island's principal cemetery, where headstones make fascinating reading. Many of those in the old section of the cemetery, from convict times, bear testimony to the island's violent past—its murders, mutinies, and hangings. The new portion of the cemetery con-

ABOVE: St. Barnabas Chapel was the religious center of the Melanesian Mission, which had its headquarters on Norfolk Island for over half a century. BELOW: The Norfolk Island cemetery contains reminders of the island's bloody past.

tains many stones bearing the familiar Pitcairn and *Bounty* names.

Just up a little hill from the cemetery is Bloody Bridge, which according to popular tradition was the site of the murder of a guard who was supervising its construction. Near the airport another large stone construction is The Arches, a high wall containing ten large arched openings eight or nine feet high and of equal width. Although one prevalent story states that it was constructed as a stable, it is probably also the ruin of another prisoners' barracks.

St. Barnabas Chapel, the religious center of the Melanesian Mission, lies not far from the west end of the airfield. Built as a memorial to a Melanesian Mission bishop who was killed by natives in the Solomon Islands and dedicated in 1880, it is an unexpected piece of architecture on this remote island. Above its finely-made stone walls rises a steep wooden roof, and in the gable over the entrance are a row of stained-glass panels and a large rose window. At the other end of the chapel, behind the altar, are five stained-glass windows designed by Sir Edward Burne-Jones, a famous nineteenth-century English artist. A wide aisle with a patterned floor of black marble slabs separated by white marble strips runs the length of the church, with three rows of pews on each side facing the aisle. Especially striking are the mother-of-pearl inlays (fashioned by the Melanesians who came to the Mission to study) in the pews and the woodcarving.

The Norfolk Island pine is one of the world's most beautiful trees, outstanding for its symmetry, straightness, and size: a big one can reach well over a hundred feet in height and six feet in diameter at the base. It cannot withstand a cold climate, but has been introduced into many of the warmer parts of the world, including Australia and Hawaii. Although the huge pines were everywhere at the time of Cook's discovery, they have been cut down in many areas to provide timber and to clear land for agriculture. Much of the island today resembles a large park, with small clusters and groves of pines separated by grazing land.

Old-time Norfolk Islanders live in small wooden cottages

made of the local pine. The Polynesian strain in their ancestry is difficult to see; their features are more European than anything else, and their skins are no darker than those of any European who spends a good deal of his life outdoors.

What do the Norfolk Islanders do for a living? Although water supply is sometimes a problem, the soil is fertile, and the climate allows the cultivation of tropical crops such as bananas, pineapples, coffee, papayas, and passion fruit, as well as corn, beans, sweet potatoes, potatoes, tomatoes, and onions. The Norfolk Islanders raise almost all of their own farm products and in addition catch their own fish from the surrounding ocean. They have not the area to produce large-scale agricultural exports, although for a number of years the chief source of income was derived from raising various seeds, particularly bean seed, for export to Australia and New Zealand.

Another export, whale oil, has completely ceased. Whales, which used to appear in the surrounding waters at certain seasons of the year, were killed by hardy Norfolk Islanders in open boats and towed to land for processing. After World War II, a modern whaling factory was constructed, but it was abandoned in the early 1960's because the nearby waters no longer had whales in sufficient numbers.

The job opportunities lost to the people of Norfolk when seed production dropped and whaling ceased have been more than made up by a rapid rise in tourism since 1960. The island's scenic beauty, quiet, and historic sites are obvious attractions, but of additional importance has been Norfolk's status as the nearest duty-free port to New Zealand and Australia. The savings on watches, cameras, television sets, stereo equipment, radios, and the like—most of them manufactured in Japan and Hong Kong—will help pay for a Norfolk Island vacation. All of Norfolk's imports except those arriving by air must be transferred in large boats from ships lying half a mile offshore, often through treacherous seas. Each automobile and piece of heavy equipment on the island, as well as much of the merchandise in the duty-free stores, pays tribute to the boat-handling skill of the sturdy men of Norfolk.

As the result of the absence of taxes on Norfolk, the island became a haven for commercial enterprises, which could operate tax-free by establishing Norfolk as their nominal headquarters. One report states that between 1964 and 1971 the number of companies registered on the island soared from twenty to over fifteen hundred. All of this "business" brings an income to a few accounting and law offices and to a small number of islanders who serve (in name at least) as directors and shareholders of the firms. In 1971 a committee of the Australian Senate was working on an ordinance which would put tighter controls on Norfolk Island companies. If restrictions become too great, many such companies might jump to other Pacific island tax havens, such as the New Hebrides or the tiny island republic of Nauru. Old-time Norfolk Islanders lament the commercialism which outsiders have brought to their once placid community, as well as the possibility that Norfolk may for the first time become included in Australia's tax levies.

The old Norfolk families still have a considerable heritage from the *Bounty*. This consists of interrelationship and a feeling of solidarity rather than any collection of material objects. (However, the old stew kettle from the *Bounty*, minus fragments carried away over the years by souvenir hunters, occupies an important place in the island's museum.) While they speak standard English in everyday dealings with other people, among themselves the *Bounty* descendants use a unique dialect which is mostly derived from that of their English ancestors, but which has certain words of Tahitian origin for the names of objects, plants, and foods.

That the youngsters are aware of their history and of their cousins four thousand miles away was evident in a visit to Norfolk Island's neat little Central School, which has between two and three hundred students. For their next composition the pupils in one grade had been assigned the subject "Life on Pitcairn."

Down Under to
New Zealand

Auckland, New Zealand, lies almost exactly as far away from the equator (though on the other side) as San Francisco or Washington, D.C. Most of the islands of Polynesia are generally warm, but it is winter in New Zealand during June, July, and August. Actually most of New Zealand has a very temperate climate; at Auckland the low temperatures in the winter months average thirty-seven degrees and the high temperatures in the summer average in the low eighties. And snow falls rarely in Auckland—about as often as it does in New Orleans. At its extremes, New Zealand climate ranges from subtropical in the north to pretty cool in the south. Of inhabited countries in the Southern Hemisphere, only the tips of Chile and Argentina lie farther south.

Geographically, New Zealand is the most isolated country of any size in the world. The nearest continents are Australia and Antarctica; Asia and the Americas are five to ten thousand miles away, and Europe is on the other side of the globe.

Except for some small islands under its control, New Zealand consists of two principal islands, each about five hundred miles long and one hundred miles wide at the widest. With imagination, one can see that the North Island looks like a distorted fish with its mouth open attempting to devour the South Island—an ambitious task, since the South Island is bigger. The two islands together are about the same size as the state of Colorado, or a little larger than England, Scotland, and Wales together, or about seven-tenths the size of Japan.

New Zealand has a population of about 2,860,000, close to that of Iowa or Connecticut. Nearly seventy percent of these people live on the North Island. Over a million and a quarter people live in the four largest cities. In the North Island, Auckland has about 600,000 in its urban area; Wellington, the capital, has about half as many if the population of Hutt, its twin city, is included. In the South Island, Christchurch has about a quarter of a million residents and Dunedin over 100,000. Of the entire population the largest group is of European, principally British, ancestry, but a sizeable group is of Maori (the New Zealand Polynesian) blood.

Anthropologists are still searching for the answers concerning the first inhabitants of New Zealand. Apparently an early group of settlers arrived about A.D. 1000, probably from the Society Islands, well over two thousand miles away. New Zealand originally had no mammals other than bats, but contained a large number of birds, including several varieties incapable of flight. The largest of these was the *moa*, something like a gigantic ostrich, whose bones indicate that it was up to twelve feet tall. The early Polynesian immigrants apparently found the *moa* an excellent source of food, particularly on the South Island, where the birds flourished in greater numbers. This period of ancient New Zealand life is called the "Moa-Hunter period." So efficient were the Moa-Hunters in their technique that the birds became rarer and rarer and probably were extinct by 1600.

Contact with Central Polynesia was lost for several centuries, although traditions indicate that a voyager who returned to Tahiti kept alive the knowledge of a great new land two thousand miles to the southwest. Maori traditions further state that about 1350 a fleet of seven or eight huge canoes from Tahiti brought settlers to New Zealand. The story of how the new

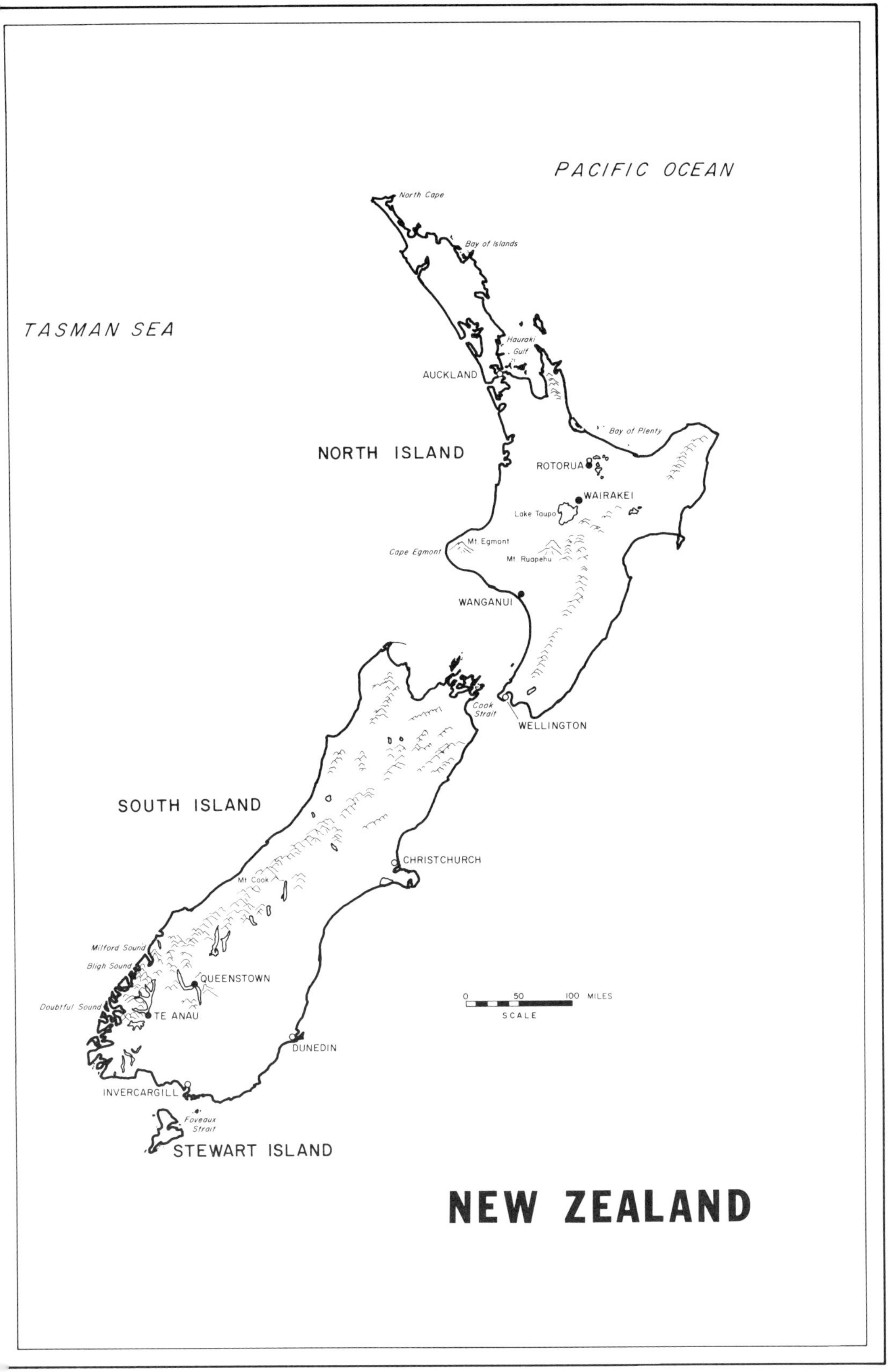

PACIFIC OCEAN

TASMAN SEA

North Cape

Bay of Islands

Hauraki
Gulf

AUCKLAND

NORTH ISLAND

Bay of Plenty

ROTORUA

WAIRAKEI

Lake Taupo

Cape Egmont

Mt Egmont

Mt Ruapehu

WANGANUI

Cook
Strait

WELLINGTON

SOUTH ISLAND

Mt Cook

CHRISTCHURCH

Milford Sound

Bligh Sound

Doubtful Sound

QUEENSTOWN

TE ANAU

0   50   100 MILES
SCALE

DUNEDIN

INVERCARGILL

Foveaux
Strait

STEWART ISLAND

NEW ZEALAND

settlers conquered or assimilated the older settlers is obscure. Indeed, some scientists doubt that the "great migration" as described in tradition ever took place. It is clear that the inhabitants' way of life changed greatly over several hundred years— the people became fishers and agriculturists, for example—but this evolution could have resulted from the killing off of the *moa*, rather than from the introduction of a new culture. On the other hand, even if no great fleet actually arrived at New Zealand, over the centuries following the first settlement, occasional canoeloads of lost or exploring Polynesians could well have landed in New Zealand.

However they had been imported, the Polynesian customs and way of life underwent a great transformation in this new, different environment. With a large land mass available the people gave up seafaring and over the years became principally landsmen. Of the three important Polynesian animals—the pig, dog, and chicken—apparently only the dog came with them. The Polynesian staple plants of coconut, breadfruit, and banana —if they were brought—didn't grow, though the sweet potato did. Besides being hard on the plants, the cool climate must have been a considerable shock to the tropical Polynesians, and they invented new, warmer garments using the fibers of the native flax.

The Maoris developed an architecture which provided warmer houses, and although they did not build great stone temples as did many other Polynesians, they built large meeting houses. A characteristic of Maori architecture is the use of elaborate decorative carving, the finest in the Pacific. On the South Island they found jade from which they fashioned "greenstone" tools, short war clubs, and ornaments. Fantastic tattoos involving curved and spiral lines decorated the faces of chiefs.

The Maori tribes engaged in extensive warfare, often over desirable areas of land, but more importantly because war was a favorite activity; victory in battle was the highest honor a tribe could win. The Maoris became skilful military engineers, building fortified villages, or *pa*, usually on hilltops, surrounded by palisades, terraces, and ditches.

The name "New Zealand" is of Dutch origin; the Maori name is Autearoa, "Land of the Long White Cloud." Abel Tasman, the Dutch explorer, was the first European to sight New Zealand, in 1642. He lost four men in a skirmish with Maoris who came out in canoes from the South Island, and he decided not to try landing on the North Island when the Maoris there also seemed hostile. Over a century and a quarter passed before the next European, Captain Cook, arrived. He charted the entire coastline of the two islands and discovered the fifteen-mile-wide Cook Strait, which Tasman had missed, separating them. Although he had a few scuffles, he was generally successful in dealing with the Maoris. On at least one stop, Cook noted evidence of cannibalism.

In the early nineteenth century, whalers and sealers found New Zealand a convenient stopping place, and European settlement began. The first mission station was established by the Reverend Samuel Marsden in 1814. It was a Christianized chief, the great Tamati Waka Nene, who encouraged other chiefs to sign the Treaty of Waitangi in February, 1840, by which the Maoris officially accepted British sovereignty, receiving in return British protection and guaranteed possession of certain lands and fisheries. Organized colonization of New Zealand began that year.

Over the next twenty-five years, however, rebellious Maori chiefs led a series of bloody uprisings, principally over the question of land. The Maoris fought fiercely and well; they had been supplied with firearms for years, and they enjoyed warfare. In one battle, when the forces of the Crown ran out of ammunition, the Maoris offered to share ammunition so that the fight could continue on even terms.

The last big battle of the Maori wars was in 1864. Since then the Maoris and Europeans—or *pakeha*—have lived in mutual respect and relative harmony. The Maoris have full political and social rights and status, though the *pakeha*s outnumber the Maoris by about thirteen to one and possess a corresponding amount of the land. Wars, introduced diseases, and other causes reduced the Maori population to a low of 42,000 in 1896, but since then the Maori birth rate (nearly twice that of other New Zealanders) has brought the Maori population (those of at least half Maori blood) to over 225,000 in 1970.

What do you call a citizen of New Zealand? "New Zealander" is all right, but "En Zedder" is more frequently heard. ("Zed," rather than "zee," is the British way of pronouncing the name of the last letter of the alphabet.) A nickname for a New Zealander is "Kiwi," the name of one of the country's flightless birds. Rarely seen, this chicken-sized bird emerges at night from burrows in the ground to look for worms and insects. Related to the gigantic extinct *moa*, it looks hairy rather than feathery, has a long bill, and lays—for its size—a tremendous egg weighing over a pound.

New Zealand is a gorgeous country. James Michener said it "is probably the most beautiful on earth." Pete Wimberly, a Honolulu architect who has traveled all over the Pacific designing hotels, said, "If you tried to design a country for tourism with all the prime elements, including varied climate, everything from tropical to mountain scenery, fishing from deep sea to mountain streams, excellent hunting—plus skiing in August— you would come up with something like New Zealand." New Zealand is green, even in winter, except for the snow-covered mountains (especially in the South Island). A good annual rainfall and the moderate climate provide lush pastures for sheep and cattle.

New Zealand's economy is principally agricultural, with wool, meat, and dairy products accounting for over eighty-five percent of her exports. In the mid-1960's there were over fifty-one million sheep in the country, nearly twenty sheep per person. The entire United States has only about half that number. No wonder New Zealand is the world's largest exporter of mutton and lamb. New Zealand's excellent butter, cheeses, and frozen beef are shipped all over the Pacific and to England. Strawberries, apples, and "kiwi berries" (a large, fuzzy fruit larger than a lemon) are also exported in small quantities.

Although huge areas of the native forest were cut down to clear pasture land, New Zealand began an extensive and efficiently managed reforestation program in the 1920's. Many evergreens introduced from North America, such as the Monterey pine, grow more rapidly in New Zealand than in their own country, and today New Zealand's forests are among her more important resources. One of the native trees, the slow-growing kauri pine, extremely strong and durable, has unfortunately become scarce. For a time during the last century, the kauri forests provided one of the world's most unusual trades: gum digging. Over the years, gum dripping from these trees collected in lumps which eventually hardened and became buried by leaf mold and soil. This gum was found to be valuable in lacquers and varnishes. Gum diggers roamed the forests or sites of former forests probing the ground to locate these lumps, some as big as a man's head.

Not only imported trees, but wildlife—deer, wild pigs, game

A flock of sheep graze on a farm in Waitui, Inglewood, Taranaki.

birds, and trout—have been introduced and have thrived re-markably in their new home. An average New Zealand trout weighs three and a half pounds. The various species of deer have become such pests that there is no closed season or limit on them. Deer hunting is not only a sport; government hunters work for the New Zealand Forest Service, and private profes-sional hunters receive a bounty for deer.

Aside from the processing of agricultural and forest products, New Zealand's industrial development has been slow. Some machinery is manufactured, and certain types of vehicles are assembled from parts made overseas. Since New Zealand does not manufacture standard automobiles, and furthermore must carefully watch its balance of trade, automobiles are imported on a very limited quota. A New Zealander must get on a waiting list to buy a new one. As a result, some rare old cars are still chugging bravely about the countryside.

Several projects will soon boost New Zealand's industrial out-put. One is an aluminum smelter which will turn out ingots for both domestic use and export. The country's first steel mill can perhaps fill most of New Zealand's steel needs from local ores within ten years. In the North Island, natural gas and sulfur have been located in quantities which may be commercially valuable. In early 1969 the announcement was made of the first poten-tially big oil strike, a two-mile deep well in 360 feet of water, thirty-three miles offshore. These mineral resources and indus-tries, if they meet expectations, can save New Zealand between one and two million dollars in foreign exchange. Two other developing industries, fisheries and tourism, will also help the country's tight economy.

New Zealand is a member of the Commonwealth, and thus Queen Elizabeth is the nominal head of state. She is represented by a governor-general (who does not govern), appointed for a five-year term. The Parliament has one house, consisting of eighty members, of which four are directly elected by the Maori people. The Prime Minister and other cabinet ministers are chosen by the political party holding a majority in Parliament.

In 1935, as a result of the Great Depression, New Zealand,

previously always politically conservative, made a great shift and began the development of a welfare state, which has greatly changed the society. Cradle-to-grave medical services and pensions for the sick and aged are only part of the state program. The government also controls such areas as transportation, banking, communications, electricity, the tourist industry, and especially labor. Most New Zealanders are on a rigid, forty-hour, five-day week. By law all but a few of the most basic offices and businesses are locked up tightly on Saturday and Sunday. A shop owner must adhere to the hours set by the government even if he is the sole owner and employee. One effect of these regulations has been a labor shortage, indicated by large "help wanted" sections in the newspapers. The welfare state imposes a fairly high social security tax, as well as an income tax with rates generally higher than those in the United States. Wages are low; about three thousand dollars per year is average for wage earners in all classes, including the professional.

In spite of her isolation, New Zealand has taken an increasing interest in international matters. In World War I she sent nearly one hundred thousand men overseas with the Australia and New Zealand Army Corps (the famous ANZACs). One out of six lost his life. An even greater number of New Zealanders (135,000) served overseas in World War II, many of them having already departed for Europe and Africa when Japan brought the war to the Pacific. Although New Zealand's strongest ties are with other Commonwealth countries, she was a founder of the United Nations and is a member of the Southeast Asia Treaty Organization. The strong bonds formed between New Zealand and America in the Pacific struggle are still felt, and are one reason for increased postwar trade and mutual interest between the two countries. Japan has also formed economic ties with New Zealand and is now her fourth largest customer.

One New Zealander, Dr. William Cameron, regrets that in the past New Zealand has not taken a bigger part in the development of the Pacific islands to the north. With her own large Polynesian population, she seems well fitted for such a role, and still might undertake it. Although the Polynesians of the past were great travelers and emigrants, Dr. Cameron states that "the greatest migration in Polynesian history is now taking place" with thousands coming to New Zealand from Samoa, the Cook Islands, and other parts of Polynesia.

New Zealanders are an outdoor-loving people. Hunting, fishing, sailing, and skiing are popular; rugby is the most important team sport. The "All Blacks," the national rugby team (not named for the color of the players' skins) is followed keenly in its matches with other countries. Soccer, tennis, canoe racing, lawn bowling, and golf are also favorites. Finally, New Zealanders are practically fanatical about horse racing. Every city and town of consequence has at least one "racecourse."

Even though many New Zealanders today live in large cities, they have generally retained the warmth and friendliness one associates with small towns and rural people. When you make a friend of a New Zealander—which is not hard to do—you usually find that he has relatives and close friends scattered elsewhere on the two islands whom he will beg you to look up as you travel around. It's easy to get "adopted" in New Zealand.

"Kiwi" speech, in accents which an American finds quite "English," tends to be calm and straightforward. Incidentally, one should never confuse a New Zealander with an Australian, even though a few Australian sounds may be creeping into New Zealand speech. The two "down under" countries, while possessing much in common, are friendly rivals and jealously guard their national identities.

Various unfamiliar words catch an American's ear and eye. A body-and-fender repairer is called a "panelbeater"; a "hogget" has nothing to do with hogs, but is a young unshorn sheep that is no longer a lamb. But the very first thing a person needs to acquire in conversing with an En Zedder is the simple but wonderful phrase "Ah, yes!" This is used after someone answers your question, or addresses a statement to you, or at intervals while he is telling you a lengthy story. It is never used (like "Oh, yeah?") to convey doubt. It conveys appreciation, acknowledgement, interest, compassion, and a recognition that a warm common bond of humanity exists between the speaker and listener.

Auckland lies nearly halfway down the North Island of New Zealand, at a point where two harbors cut the island almost in half. The city lies between the two. The deep, important Waitemata Harbor leads east into a large gulf, an arm of the Pacific. On the west, the larger but shallower Manukau Harbor leads into the Tasman Sea. A canal only about a mile long could sever the narrowest neck of land, but a tremendous amount of dredging would be necessary to make the route useful for seagoing vessels. As a result, commercial ships from Australia go around the tip of the North Island to arrive at Waitemata.

A 3,300-foot bridge, completed in 1959, spans Waitemata Harbor, providing motor vehicles from the north ready access to downtown Auckland. The mouth of the harbor is protected by a number of offshore islands dominated by 854-foot Rang-

Aerial view from Auckland Harbor outlines Queen Street and Albert Street.

itoto, whose shape reveals it to be an extinct volcano. Within Auckland's limits rise steep, green hills which were also active volcanoes perhaps 25,000 years ago. They provided excellent sites for forts in Maori times but are parks today. A road leads to the top of the highest of these, Mount Eden (643 feet), from which there is a fine view of the city, the harbor, Rangitoto Island, and other landmarks, including One Tree Hill, which does indeed have one tree, as well as a monument, on its top. Mount Eden's summit contains a steep, grassy bowl, the crater of the old volcano. The grass both here and on the exterior hillside is kept well trimmed by sheep, which are used as "lawnmowers."

Auckland's center still contains older buildings no more than half a dozen stories high, but high-rises are replacing many such structures. New buildings are also being constructed at the University of Auckland in order to handle an expanding student body. The public universities in New Zealand's four major cities do not entirely duplicate one another, but have certain specialties in addition to providing a general program. Auckland's specialties are architecture, engineering, and fine arts.

The Domain, a large park not far from the center of the city, contains the War Memorial Museum, built to honor the dead of World War I but now honoring the dead of both World Wars. Of particular interest here is the world-famous collection of Maori material. One of the first things to strike a visitor's eye is a tremendous war canoe, eighty-three feet long, seven feet across, and capable of carrying one hundred fifty men. With the exception of a ten-foot bow section, it was hollowed out of a single huge log. Canoes of this sort, without an outrigger, were a special Maori development. At the stern an ornately carved post projects seven feet above the rest of the canoe; at the prow sits a massive carved bird.

The museum holds many other examples of Maori woodcarving—panels from houses, images, stick gods, and long war clubs. Several old Maori houses and a complete meeting house in good condition have been set up inside the museum. There are cases full of jade, or greenstone, objects, useful and ornamental. The most typical such ornament is the *hei-tiki*, a flat pendant several inches high in the form of a distorted human figure, which was a valuable heirloom. Also passed from generation to generation, accumulating the power and fame of their former owners, were greenstone clubs. Shaped like a short paddle with a sharpened blade, such clubs are between twelve and sixteen inches long and were used in hand-to-hand combat.

Other Maori artifacts are on display in great variety: woven garments of flax, feather cloaks (not quite as splendid as those from Hawaii and quite different in pattern), adzes (some with greenstone blades) and other tools, kites, mats, and baskets. Drawings, paintings, and photographs (including some of extremely ornate facial tattoos) provide a view of late eighteenth- and nineteenth-century Maori life and culture.

One can travel about in New Zealand in two ways. One way is to rent a car—remembering that in this country traffic keeps to the left. The other is to go to an office of the New Zealand Government Tourist Bureau and tell the agent exactly where and how you want to go and how long you want to stay. Within a day, usually, he will prepare a complete set of tickets—taxi, bus, train, plane, and hotel, as well as maps and information about your route. Planning is done with amazing thoroughness: if you get off a bus or train, you don't have to look for a taxi; there's a driver looking for you, by name.

To see today's Maori life, one should head south for Rotorua, about a hundred and fifty miles away. A volcanic and thermal belt, one of New Zealand's distinctive geological features, cuts diagonally across the center of the North Island. Along this belt are several active volcanoes, many old volcanic sites, and a number of geysers, bubbling mud pools, and hot springs. Lake Rotorua, over seven miles long and six miles wide, lies in this thermal belt.

The Rotorua area has been the home of Maoris for centuries; today a city of over twenty thousand has grown up between two Maori villages at the south end of the lake. In Ohinemutu Village, at the north end of the city, one finds that today Maoris don't build their houses with walls of flax latticework and thatched roofs; they use board siding and metal or shingle roofs. But the houses still have the old design: they are rectangular and have few windows in the sides. At the front, which may contain a window or two as well as the door, the roof and the side walls project to form a sort of porch. Old style carved panels may be seen along the uprights supporting this projection and on the slanting facings leading to the gable tip, which is surmounted by a carved figure. The old Maori carved panels were colored brick-red with a pigment made from clay. This red pigment was also used for painted patterns, in combination with a white clay pigment. Today hardware-store paint is probably used for convenience.

Ohinemutu doesn't have any geysers, but steam cracks and hot pools with low stone borders are everywhere. The hotter pools and steam jets provide natural cooking facilities (handy in preparing fish from the nearby lake), and some pools are

Pohutu Geyser, Whakarewarewa, Rotorua, is impressive in action.

screened off to provide families with their own private hot baths. In the center of the village a statue of Queen Victoria, scepter in hand, rests incongruously upon a post with four grinning, white-toothed faces under a Maori-style canopy, only a few feet away from a cooking vent. Not far away is a carved wooden figure with a large open mouth which goes completely through the head. In the mouth hangs a bell; the sound of the bell is the voice of the *tiki*.

The village has a noted church, with solid outside walls but a real Maori interior displaying excellent carvings and decorations. Nearby is the shop of a woodcarver, who slowly turns out panels in the old motifs, though with better tools than the stone ones his ancestors used. He regrets that it is hard to find young people who are interested in learning the art—they'd rather work in a gas station or take some other job that doesn't require so much training.

At the other Maori village, Whakarewarewa, usually called simply "Whaka," the thermal activity is more widespread and violent, including Pohutu Geyser, which throws a jet of boiling water and steam from sixty to a hundred feet into the air at irregular intervals. A fortified village, or *pa,* has been constructed near the main road at the edge of the thermal area to show the way the Maoris lived in the old days. The model *pa* is surrounded by palisades—long, slender poles, spaced so that no enemy could slip through. Over the palisades glare carved images on posts, their tongues thrust out in defiance.

The carved gateway at the entrance to the *pa* depicts a pair of legendary lovers, Tutanekai and Hinemoa, who were married in spite of parental objections. An island in the middle of the lake is associated with their story and bears a hot spring called Hinemoa's bath. Inside the *pa* are many kinds of Maori structures. One sees that a chief's house was larger than a commoner's, but both were low-ceilinged to conserve heat. Food was stored in a small house on supports to keep rats and dampness out. Birdhouses—small copies of the human dwellings—perch on tall posts. Carved images of warriors and dancers stand here and there.

Maori songs and dances are frequently performed in Rotorua. At a quick glance, the costume of the female dancers resembles the attire of southwest American Indians. The women wear bands around their heads, and their bodices have a black, red, and white diamond pattern. On top of a red underskirt they wear an unusual skirt made of flax leaves which have dried into long, thin tubes, with alternating areas of black and white along their lengths. These swish and rustle as the dancers perform. The movements are more restrained than those of most Polynesian dances; a typical motion is a rapid fluttering of the open palms. Maori women are famous for their canoe dances, which feature paddling motions, and *poi* dances. A *poi* is a light fiber ball about the size of a baseball, which is twirled during a dance on the end of a string. The string may be a foot or several feet long. Skilful *poi* twirlers can twirl four *poi* at a time, each hand keeping two going in opposite directions, in a beautiful series of gyrations. Some can also keep a fifth one going—from a big toe.

The most typical men's dance is the energetic war dance, or *haka*, in which the warrior, his face painted to represent the old tattooing, makes menacing gestures with his greenstone war club. Wild shouts and ferocious facemaking, including crossing the eyes and sticking the tongue out and downward to its farthest limit, are important parts of such a dance.

Less than fifty miles south of Rotorua is Wairakei, a thermal area where man has put nature to work to create power. Beginning in the 1950's bores were sunk, tapping superheated steam under great pressure. A system of large pipes leads the steam through separators, which remove unwanted water, and then to a power plant a mile or two away. Dozens of bores have been completed; they fill the valley with the roar of steam jets and plumy clouds of escaping steam. In 1963 this geothermal source was producing nearly 200,000 kilowatts—about one tenth of the power of all New Zealand at that time. The construction of huge hydroelectric projects in the South Island has reduced the relative importance of geothermal steam. The Wairakei region has its own hydroelectric power as well; the rushing Waikato River has been dammed for that purpose. The dam cut off the water from a spectacular, rapid-filled gorge just below, but water is released for short periods according to a regular schedule to allow visitors to see the display.

The thermal bores had an unfortunate effect on the natural phenomena in Geyser Valley, a short distance away. Before the drilling it contained several spectacular geysers, along with hot springs and bubbling mud pools of various colors and a number of fantastic natural formations. Although the rest of the sights are still worth seeing, the geysers are now very feeble.

About five miles up the Waikato River is the river's source, Lake Taupo, with the attractive town of Taupo on its shore. The largest lake in all New Zealand, Taupo is twenty-five miles long, sixteen miles wide, and has some of the world's finest fishing, both in its own waters and in the streams that feed it. The drive along its southeastern shore gives a view of blue waters, beaches, tributaries, and the hills that surround its 1,200-foot-high surface.

On toward Wellington from Lake Taupo, the road rises steadily and passes along the edge of Tongariro National Park, which surrounds the volcanic peaks of Ruapehu (9,175 feet), Ngauruhoe (7,515 feet), and Tongariro (6,517 feet). These peaks include a number of craters, some filled with small lakes. The three volcanoes are all considered active; Ngauruhoe has been by far the most active in recent years, but Ruapehu came to life in 1969. At least a half dozen glaciers extend down the upper flanks of Ruapehu, and the skiing on Ruapehu's slopes attracts winter sports lovers from all over the North Island. Chair lifts used by skiers in the winter also operate on a reduced schedule in the summer to take visitors to within two thousand feet (in elevation) of the summit.

Wanganui, on the Tasman Sea, is about eighty miles from the park. On the way one passes "Three Lakes"—really a cluster of ponds—which change their color from time to time because of water vegetation. A viewer may find one of them completely black, one a bright green, and the other green at one end and bluish-gray at the other. At certain times of the year the green turns to red. These mysterious lakes were *tapu* to the Maoris.

Wanganui, an attractive city of about 40,000, lies at the mouth of the Wanganui River. On Durie Hill, across the river from the city proper, stands a war memorial tower. Its 120-foot-high observation platform gives an outstanding view of the surrounding hills, the river, the Tasman Sea, and the city and its many parks. One of the parks has an imaginatively designed children's playground. It includes a huge metal octopus with arched tentacles, from each of which is suspended a pair of swings. The slide goes down a dinosaur's back; the gaping mouth of a huge whale provides a cave in which to play Jonah. Wanganuians are justifiably proud of their city, its museum with a good Maori collection, its art gallery, and its river. A harbor development project will improve the port's commercial importance.

Wellington is 120 miles away, at the southern tip of the North Island. Among the excellent harbors of the Pacific—San Francisco, Pago Pago, Rabaul, Manila, Hong Kong, and Sydney—Wellington ranks as one of the finest. Officially called Port Nicholson, it is a large bay that leads out to Cook Strait through a narrows not much more than a mile wide. The old part of Wellington lies west of the bay, but the city has expanded to include land that reaches around toward its southern entrance. The city of Hutt, at the back of the bay, is part of the greater Wellington area.

Hills rising not far from the waterline give Wellington something of the appearance of an older San Francisco. The similarity is increased by a cable car which goes up a steep hill behind the downtown section. At the top of the hill, in the district of Kelburn, are Wellington's beautifully landscaped Botanical Gardens.

Although Auckland is larger and probably more important industrially, Wellington's location and its place as the capital of the country have made it of greater importance in other ways. It serves as a center for both international and interisland commerce. Victoria University, the National Art Gallery, the Dominion Museum, with another outstanding Maori collection, and a library with fine Pacific materials are in Wellington; it is the home of the National Orchestra as well as opera and ballet companies.

The beer trucks on the streets and highways strike an American as unusual. New Zealanders consume large quantities of beer; keeping a dispenser supplied through cases or even kegs would be an endless task. Therefore, beer is transported in huge tank trucks, similar to gasoline or milk tankers, from which the beverage is pumped into the large storage tanks of each bar.

One of the best places to get a view of the city and harbor of Wellington is the top of Mount Victoria, 643 feet high, reached by a road which passes through a park. In one direction lie the busy harbor, the center of Wellington, and a number of hilltop residential sections. In another direction are more residential sections and, on a flat neck of land separating Port Nicholson from Cook Strait, the Wellington Airport. On Mount Victoria,

Wellington City and Harbor look toward Oriental Bay and Mt. Victoria.

New Zealand has built a memorial in honor of Admiral Richard E. Byrd, the American Antarctic explorer. Its nearness to the Antarctic has made New Zealand the base for most American and British expeditions to the bottom of the world. Cook Strait, which separates New Zealand's two main islands, lies about a dozen miles away "around the corner" from the mouth of the harbor.

Two interisland ferries leave from Wellington. One goes fifty-two miles across the strait to Picton, at the northern end of the South Island. The other goes 175 miles overnight to Lyttelton, a third the way down the east coast. In April, 1968, a Wellington-Lyttelton ferry was the victim of New Zealand's greatest sea disaster. The 490-foot *Wahine* was entering Port Nicholson in winds estimated at 125 miles per hour when it was blown onto a reef in the narrow entrance and capsized only a few miles from the dock. Of the seven hundred passengers and crewmen aboard, over fifty lost their lives. Except for the heroic rescue efforts of small-boat owners, the toll would have been much greater.

Ferry passengers are awakened by the stewardess before dawn with the standard New Zealand preface to breakfast—a cup of tea and a biscuit. Lyttelton, a small deep harbor at the base of the South Island's fin, or thumb, is actually the crater of an ancient volcano, one side of which has opened up to the sea. It is the port for the major city of Christchurch, which is separated from it by a steep mountain range. In the early days everything brought to Christchurch by sea had to be taken over a 634-foot pass. Today there are tunnels for trains and motor vehicles.

Christchurch lies at the edge of the Canterbury Plains, a fertile agricultural area of almost table flatness, a hundred miles long and up to forty miles wide. The plains are crossed at intervals by streams and rivers coming from the Southern Alps, New Zealand's highest mountains, which parallel the island's western side. The city was founded by the Canterbury Association, a group of British colonists closely associated with the Church of England. The first four shiploads of settlers—the "Canterbury Pilgrims"—arrived in late December, 1850. From the start the city was laid out in a neat rectangular pattern with a large square in the center for a cathedral. More impressive than beautiful, the massive Anglican cathedral, whose 215-foot spire dominates the heart of the city, took forty years to complete. Most cities are content with a single nickname and hope that it's favorable. Christchurch has at least five. It is called "the Cathedral City" and "City of the Plains" for obvious reasons.

Christchurch has also been called "the most English city out-side of England" (some people even go so far as to say that it's *more* English than England). The settlers tried to build their city in the image of their homeland; not only the architecture and the landscaping, but also the names of streets and other features show their determination. The city's own name is that of a fa-mous college in Oxford. Through the city winds an attractive stream, the River Avon, flanked by lawns and trees, with Oxford Terrace on one side and Cambridge Terrace on the other. Just outside the center of the city the Avon curves through a large botanical garden. The landscaping of Christchurch accounts for its other two nicknames: "City of Trees" and "Garden City."

On the banks of the Avon only a few blocks from the cathedral stands a larger-than-life statue of Captain Robert F. Scott, made by his sculptress wife. Hoping to be the first man in history to reach the South Pole, Scott arrived in January, 1912, to find that the Norwegian explorer Roald Amundsen had been there five weeks earlier. Scott and four companions perished in Antarctica in 1912 on the trek back.

With about a third of the population of the South Island living in or near Christchurch, the city serves as a kind of capital for the island. Its university, which also includes an agricultural college some miles distant, is older than those of Auckland and Wellington.

A rather unusual vehicle makes the eight-hour drive to Mount Cook National Park in the Southern Alps. It is built like a bus but has seats for only about a dozen passengers in the forward section; the whole aft end is a cavern holding freight and bag-gage. Along part of the route the driver pauses to deliver parcels to isolated farms.

Cathedral and square, Christchurch City, Canterbury, bring old England to New Zealand.

Traveling the length of the Canterbury Plains, the bus crosses several bridges which seem extremely long for the width of the streams below (when winter snows melt in the uplands these streams become raging rivers). Finally it turns toward the mountains, crossing the first range through a 2,200-foot pass and descending into the MacKenzie Basin.

The South Island has a number of long, narrow lakes, carved by prehistoric glaciers. We pass the tip of one of these, fifteen-mile-long Lake Tekapo; its half-mile high waters are surrounded during the winter months by snow-clad mountains. From certain points on the highway one can see Mount Cook in the distance.

Mount Cook National Park, established in 1952, contains twenty-two peaks over 10,000 feet high. It also has a number of glaciers, including the eighteen-mile-long Tasman Glacier, half again as long as any in Switzerland. The Hermitage, the National Park hotel, draws sightseers, hikers, hunters, mountaineers, and other sportsmen the year round. Skiing is normally good during the four winter months.

Above and around The Hermitage rise the Southern Alps. Their glaciers, icefalls, and rugged sides with bare cliffs punctuating the snow remind one that this was the training ground for Sir Edmund Hillary, the first conqueror of Mount Everest and the first man after Captain Scott to reach the South Pole by land. Mount Cook looks the way a mountain should—sharply pointed, majestic, and dangerous. It deserves its Maori name, Aorangi, the Cloud-Piercer. Actually Hawaii's Mauna Loa and Mauna Kea are more than ten percent higher than Mount Cook, but their greater bulk and more gradual slopes make them much less dramatic. The sun leaves the valley early in the afternoon but continues to light the upper parts of the Alps, finally bathing the snow in a post-sunset pink light.

Ski plane skims over the Ball Glacier in the Southern Alps.

To the south, 190 miles by road from The Hermitage, is Queenstown, on the shores of fifty-two-mile-long Lake Wakatipu. Queenstown is of historic importance in connection with New Zealand's gold rush. Although small amounts of gold were found in New Zealand in the late 1850's, the gold rush started with big strikes in the mountains near Queenstown in 1862. Eager prospectors came from the gold fields of California and Australia and from more remote parts of the world as word spread. The gold boom eventually ended, but it played an important part in populating New Zealand (its population nearly tripled in a half dozen years) and in furnishing money for its development. Today less than a million dollars worth of gold is mined per year in all New Zealand.

Following cliff-clinging trails and narrow roads along the valleys near Queenstown one can find the remains of mining sites and ghost towns, some of which once had over a thousand inhabitants. Queenstown is now a thriving vacation center, offering boating, fishing, hunting, hiking, mountain climbing, and visits to the historic gold fields. In winter, Coronet Peak, a mile high, furnishes some of New Zealand's best skiing, even drawing ski enthusiasts from the northern half of the world who have grown impatient with their summer. Summer or winter, the chair lift to the top of Coronet Peak provides a fine view of the Queenstown area, including a range of mile-and-a-half-high mountains rising from the lake which are called The Remarkables, and are.

The bus south out of Queenstown follows the lake for about twenty-five miles along the lower slopes of The Remarkables. The lake is no more than three miles wide, but is nearly a quarter of a mile deep. Across its blue waters rise other mountains. Nearly ninety miles farther south is Te Anau, an attractive town on a lake of the same name. On the way a slight delay may be caused by a small army of several thousand sheep being moved along the road to a new pasture.

Though not as long as Lake Wakatipu, Lake Te Anau, with its three large branches, or fiords, covers the largest area of any lake in the South Island and is second in all New Zealand to the

North Island's Taupo. Much of Te Anau is surrounded by a thick wilderness, or "bush," as New Zealanders call it, some of it virtually unexplored. About twenty years ago, in a valley west of the lake, a surprising discovery was made: a group of *takahe,* birds which are flightless like the *kiwi* but larger and more beautiful. The species had been thought extinct for half a century; their habitat is now protected by law.

While much of the South Island has a narrow coastal plain along the Tasman Sea, with scattered towns connected by a main road, the lower quarter of this coast is very mountainous and deeply indented by more than a dozen fiordlike inlets bearing such names as Milford Sound, Bligh Sound, Dusky Sound, and Doubtful Sound. At Te Anau this coast lies on the other side of the mountains to the west. Milford Sound, considered the most spectacular of all, can be reached from Te Anau by foot, motor vehicle, or plane.

A launch to the upper end of the lake takes one to the end of Milford Track ("track" is the New Zealanders' word for "trail"), a thirty-three-mile, three-day hike which has been called one of the world's outstanding walks. The track goes through a high pass between 7,000-foot mountains. The newer vehicular road uses an entirely different pass, with a tunnel at its summit. Planes provide the only way of crossing the mountains when both passes are blocked by winter snow. Milford Track climbs up a valley, then zigzags through a pass. Beyond the summit is Sutherland Falls, which drop an awesome 1,900 feet out of Lake Quill.

A fine hotel stands at the head of Milford Sound, and through the picture window of the lobby one can look down the narrow inlet, on the left side of which imposing Mitre Peak rises sharply over 5,500 feet. On the right, The Lion is lower, but steeper.

Manapouri, considered New Zealand's most beautiful lake, with several dozen islands beneath a background of snowy mountains, deserves a visit. Many of the South Island's high lakes have already been used as reservoirs for hydroelectric power plants, and development of this resource is continuing. The government's Manapouri project, which has employed a

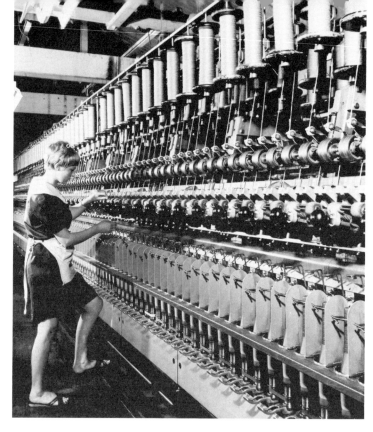

Uniflex spinning frame, Mosgiel Woollens Ltd., Dunedin, makes an eloquent statement for modern industry.

number of American engineers, will be the largest of all, and is rapidly nearing completion. It will be the chief power source for New Zealand's forthcoming aluminum industry.

Hill-surrounded Dunedin, New Zealand's fourth largest city, lies toward the bottom of the east side of the South Island. Even as Christchurch was founded by a group of religious-minded Englishmen, Dunedin was founded by a similar group of Scotsmen, in the 1840's. Today it is considered the most Scottish city outside of Scotland, and Robert Burns, honored by a statue, is held in great esteem. Its name was originally intended to be New Edinburgh, but finally the old Gaelic name for Edinburgh was used. As the gateway port during New Zealand's gold rush, the city grew rapidly, and the hard-working inhabitants continued to develop successful enterprises as the gold boom faded. Its university is the oldest in the country (1869), and its Early Settlers'

Museum contains fascinating exhibits showing the dress, transportation, and manner of living in the pioneer and gold-rush days.

Over a hundred miles further to the south is Invercargill, New Zealand's southernmost important city and port, with a heritage both Scottish and Irish. Across a seventeen-mile strait toward the pole from New Zealand's southeast tip lies Stewart Island, a roughly triangular island twenty-five or thirty miles on a side. The strait is the source of New Zealand's finest oysters, and the island is a favorite nesting place for the mutton bird. The young of this sea bird, a kind of puffin, are pulled from underground burrows and sold as food throughout New Zealand. The fat meat of the mutton bird tastes like a combination of fowl and fish.

The government-operated railway runs a main line all the way up the east side of the South Island. The eight-hour train ride from Dunedin to Christchurch provides fine and varied scenery of both seacoast and farmland. New Zealanders are great ones for keeping passenger lists; both on buses and trains which go any distance the ticket taker has a complete roster of passengers on which he faithfully checks off each passenger's name.

The trains have no dining cars, but on the way up the coast there are "tea stops" of a half dozen minutes and two "meal stops," about twice as long. The minute the train comes to a halt the passengers dash to the refreshment counter and emerge triumphantly clutching cups of tea, hot pies (with meat filling), cake, fruit, and sandwiches, which they take aboard the train. The empty cups are picked up at the next stop. A New Zealand sandwich consists of bread that has been sliced to incredible thinness, a generous lather of New Zealand's justly famous butter, and a faintly discernible filling, which may surprise an American by consisting of spaghetti or creamed corn.

After returning to Wellington on the overnight ferry, it is interesting to drive back to Auckland using a largely different route. The big peninsula on the west side of North Island is Cape Egmont, with 8,260-foot Mount Egmont in its center. Egmont is a beautiful, nearly symmetrical, volcanic cone which has not been active in 250 years. It is New Zealand's equivalent of Mount Shasta, Rainier, or Fujiyama.

Just north of the Egmont peninsula is a memorial honoring Sir Peter Buck, or Te Rangi Hiroa, who in himself joined New Zealand's two important races and cultures. Born in 1880 of a Maori mother and an Irish father, Buck earned a medical degree and did outstanding medical work among the Maori people. However, he developed a strong interest in Pacific anthropology, and for the last twenty-four years of his life, until his death in 1951, was a staff member and then director of the Bishop Museum in Honolulu.

Finally, about 130 miles south of Auckland is Waitomo, where pathways, steps, and lighting have made several large limestone caverns convenient for visitors. The chief feature is the glowworm grotto above a large pool in an underground stream. The glowworm, actually the larva of a kind of fly which dwells in the cave, lives in a mucus tube attached to the cave's roof. It lowers several sticky threads into space to entangle its food—small flying insects attracted by the glowworm's light. The larvae exist in many parts of the cave and in other New Zealand caves as well, but they are in special profusion in the grotto. Visitors move into the grotto in a rowboat in complete darkness and see absolutely nothing—the eyes need time to adjust. Then slowly a faint blue glow becomes apparent in hundreds, then thousands, then tens of thousands of tiny spots. It is as if the roof had suddenly disappeared and the stars of a new sky—an insect-made planetarium—had taken its place.

A visitor finds it hard to leave beautiful New Zealand. As a farewell to the pleasant "En Zedders," a little song might be adapted:

> So here's to friendly New Zealand,
> Where the sheep and the *kiwi* abound;
> Where seldom is heard a discouraging word,
> Though the map has a Doubtful Sound.

(Doubtful can be located on the map about sixty miles south of Milford Sound.)

The Fiftieth State

Mark Twain never forgot Hawaii. In 1889, in a speech to a baseball team that had visited Hawaii, he said:

> No alien land in all the world has any deep, strong charm for me but that one, no other land could so longingly and so beseechingly haunt me sleeping and waking, through half a lifetime, as that one has done. Other things leave me, but it abides; other things change, but it remains the same. For me its balmy airs are always blowing, its summer seas flashing in the sun; the pulsing of its surf-beat is in my ear; I can see its garlanded crags, its leaping cascades, its plumy palms drowsing by the shore, its remote summits floating like islands above the cloud rack; I can feel the spirit of its woodland solitudes, I can hear the plash of its brooks; in my nostrils still lives the breath of flowers that perished twenty years ago.

Visitors have been charmed by the beautiful islands as long as their history has been recorded. The first European visitors found Hawaii beautiful but not always peaceful.

At the time of Hawaii's discovery by Captain Cook in 1778, the various islands were under the control of high chiefs, or *ali'i*, who were of royal descent but often had to maintain their rights in battle against rival *ali'i* of the same or other islands. Kamehameha, a chief born in the north part of the island of Hawaii, who was about twenty at the time of Cook's visit, was the first leader to bring all the main islands under one rule. His conquest was aided by cannon, muskets, and a few foreigners from vessels which followed Cook's to the islands. By 1795 Kamehameha was acknowledged king by all but the northern islands of Kauai and Niihau, and the period of Hawaiian monarchy began.

Kamehameha I ("The Great") was succeeded by four successive descendants who also assumed the name Kamehameha, which means "The Lonely One." Kamehameha II (Liholiho) ruled from 1819 to 1824; both he and his queen died of measles on a visit to London in 1824. Liholiho's younger brother became Kamehameha III at the age of nine and ruled until his death in 1854, the longest reign of any of the Hawaiian kings. His nephews, the last two Kamehamehas, ruled nine years each. After the death of Kamehameha V in 1873, three later monarchs were elected by the Legislative Assembly from among highly eligible *ali'i:* Lunalilo (1873–1874), Kalakaua (1874–1891), and Queen Liliuokalani (1891–1893).

But the history of Hawaii is more than just who ruled. The early 1800's brought seafaring visitors in the China trade, and ships called with increasing frequency. Later the whalers found Hawaii a mid-Pacific haven. Hawaii's flag, adopted in 1816, looks like a combination of the British and American flags, thereby showing two important outside influences.

The foreigners brought new diseases to which large numbers of Hawaiians, lacking natural immunity, succumbed in successive epidemics. Cook had estimated that the islands were inhabited by 300,000 Hawaiians, but this may well have been an overestimate. The estimated population of over 150,000 in 1800 dropped by 1872 to a low ebb of fewer than 57,000, of whom about ninety percent were Hawaiians and part-Hawaiians. Thereafter the *overall* population grew rather rapidly, but the percentage of Hawaiians continued to decline. Probably fewer than 5,000 pure Hawaiians are living today, although there are over 100,000 part-Hawaiians as a result of intermarriage.

The foreigners also brought new practices and ideas, many of which supplanted native customs and beliefs. Though

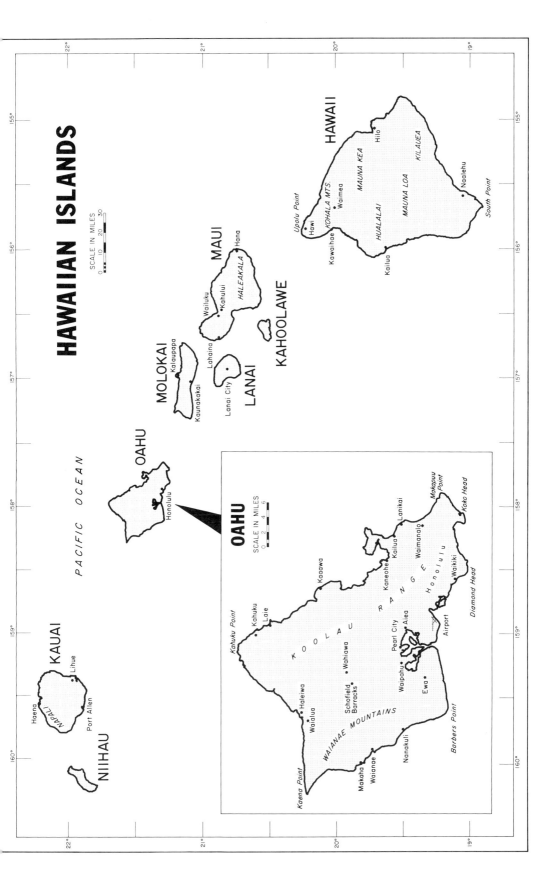

HAWAIIAN ISLANDS

SCALE IN MILES
0 10 20 30

PACIFIC OCEAN

NIIHAU

KAUAI
Haena
NAPALI
Lihue
Port Allen

OAHU
Honolulu

MOLOKAI
Kalaupapa
Kaunakakai

LANAI
Lanai City

Lahaina

MAUI
Wailuku
Kahului
HALEAKALA
Hana

KAHOOLAWE

HAWAII
Upolu Point
Hawi
Kawaihae
KOHALA MTS.
Waimea
Hilo
MAUNA KEA
HUALALAI
MAUNA LOA
KILAUEA
Kailua
Naalehu
South Point

OAHU

SCALE IN MILES
0 2 4 6

Kahuku Point
Kahuku
Laie
Kaaawa

K O O L A U   R A N G E

Kaneohe
Kailua
Lanikai
Waimanalo
Makapuu Point
Koko Head

Haleiwa
Waialua
Schofield Barracks
Wahiawa
Pearl City
Aiea
Waipahu
Ewa

Honolulu
Waikiki
Airport
Diamond Head

Kaena Point
Makaha
Waianae
WAIANAE MOUNTAINS
Nanakuli
Barbers Point

Kamehameha the Great remained faithful to the religion of his forefathers, which included a complicated system of *kapus* (or *tabus*), his successor, Liholiho, publicly violated a *kapu* dealing with eating to show that the old system was overthrown. Shortly thereafter, in 1820, the first group of Protestant missionaries arrived from New England via Cape Horn to start filling the religious vacuum and to help in education, medicine, agriculture, and the establishment of "morality." The New Englanders put the Hawaiian language into written form and printed the first Hawaiian books. In representing the Hawaiian sounds, the missionaries used only the five vowels and seven consonants (*h, k, l, m, n, p,* and *w*), although the language probably had several more sounds than these dozen letters represent. It is a quite musical language; there cannot be two successive consonants, and every word ends in a vowel.

The agriculture of the early Hawaiians involved a limited number of plants and animals—taro, coconuts, bananas, sweet potatoes, yams, pigs, chickens, and dogs. After the discovery by Cook, various other plants, animals, and agricultural techniques were introduced. Sugarcane, a plant which the old Hawaiians grew just to chew on, had its commercial beginnings on Kauai in 1835 and became the first successful large-scale crop. The expanding sugar industry created a great demand for labor, which the Hawaiians could not fill, and the importation of large groups of plantation workers from many parts of the world was a principal cause of the interesting ethnic make-up of Hawaii today.

The Chinese came first, mostly between 1852 and 1883. In 1868 the first Japanese workers arrived. Later in the century came Portuguese from the Atlantic Islands. The principal groups to arrive in the twentieth century were Puerto Ricans, Koreans, and, largest of all, Filipinos. Although many of these workers served out their contracts and returned to their home countries, others liked Hawaii and stayed. The usual progress was from the plantation to the town or city, from field work to shopkeeping or a trade, and thence on up the social and economic ladder. In 1972 Hawaii's two Representatives and two

Senators were descendants of such immigrants—three of them of Japanese ancestry and one of Chinese.

Throughout most of the nineteenth century Hawaii remained politically independent, although foreign influences became more important, and at one time or another forces of Russia and France seemed about to seize the islands. The British flag actually flew over Hawaii for a few months in 1843. The idea of annexation by the United States, largely for commercial reasons, was promoted in the years following 1850 by the growing number of Americans who had taken up residence in Hawaii, and various treaties established a closer Hawaiian-American relationship.

Under the monarchy a series of constitutions increasingly liberalized the structure of the government. Nonetheless, the last monarch, Liliuokalani, desired to strengthen the power of the throne and thereby brought about the bloodless revolution which deposed her in 1893. A provisional government, which operated for less than a year and a half, established the Republic of Hawaii, which lasted until 1900. Essentially, both the provisional government and the republic were temporary stages leading to annexation by the United States. Although the annexation was formally effected in August of 1898, the Organic Act, establishing territorial status for Hawaii, was not passed until April, 1900.

From 1900 to 1959 Hawaii was the most noted example of taxation without representation under the American flag; Hawaii's hundreds of thousands of American citizens paid all federal taxes but could not vote in presidential elections and had only a voteless delegate in Washington. Hawaii's governor was appointed by the President, not elected by the people.

Statehood was slow in coming for a number of reasons. At first many legislators in Washington simply lacked interest in Hawaii and her people. Later, politically important men expressed a variety of fears, many of them based on ignorance but some the result of political calculation: fear that Hawaii's people were backward, that they were not sufficiently "Americanized," that they were not really loyal to the United States, that they might include Communists, that Congressmen from Hawaii would be Republicans or civil rightists or against the oil or beet sugar interests. Some flatly declared that no new area should be made a state which was not physically joined to the existing forty-eight.

Two world wars proved the loyalty of Hawaii's citizens. After Japan attacked Pearl Harbor on December 7, 1941, the loyalty of those of Japanese background was particularly questioned; they constituted at that time forty percent of the Territory's population. Official reports show that there was *no* sabotage or subversive activity by any Hawaii residents on Pearl Harbor Day or at any other time during the war. Furthermore, Americans of Japanese ancestry from Hawaii, notably in the 100th Infantry Battalion and the 442nd Combat Team, made a heroic record on the battlefield.

The two post-war presidents, Truman and Eisenhower, both favored statehood for Hawaii, as did various Congressional committees which investigated the matter. Finally the granting of statehood to Alaska in 1958 cleared the way for Hawaiian statehood the next year. Following an election for state officers and national representatives, President Eisenhower proclaimed Hawaii the fiftieth state on August 21, 1959. During the years of its new status Hawaii has boomed in population, in business, in higher education, and in cultural activity.

In 1950 the economy of Hawaii was based principally on income from military activity, sugar, pineapple, and tourism, in that order. Today all of these sources of income are larger than they were then, but tourism has grown more than twentyfold and seems destined to become the state's chief source of income. In 1967 Hawaii had its first million-tourist year; in 1970 the total passed a million and a half.

Hawaii is not an inexpensive place to live. Automobiles, television sets, corn flakes, and hundreds of other items cost California prices plus the additional shipping and handling expenses. State and local taxes paid per capita are among the highest in the nation. Land is expensive (in fact many people build houses on land that they rent but don't own), housing is short, and the cost of living is estimated to be about twenty percent higher than in Washington, D.C. The housing shortage extends even to tourists: in spite of the large number of hotel rooms, at certain times of the year a room is almost impossible to find, especially at popular Waikiki on Oahu.

Although the Hawaiian chain stretches for 1,500 miles, the seven largest (and only inhabited) islands extend for only about three hundred and fifty miles from northwest to southeast: Niihau, Kauai, Oahu, Molokai, Lanai, Maui, and Hawaii. The total land area is a little less than 6,500 square miles, making Hawaii forty-seventh in area among the fifty states; it is one-third larger than Connecticut, over three times the size of Delaware, and more than six times the size of Rhode Island. The total population of all the islands is nearly eight hundred thousand, about five times what it was in 1900. The "Big Island" of Hawaii has almost two-thirds of the total area; Oahu has about eighty per-

Hawaii's new State Capitol in Honolulu has open sides and rises to a craterlike crown.

cent of the population. Approximately one out of five residents of the state is a "new Hawaiian"—he's either moved there or been born there within the last five years.

Hawaii is situated just within the tropics, roughly between latitudes 19° north and 22½° north for the populated islands. The climate is mild, usually tempered by the natural air conditioning of the ocean and the northeast trade winds. For most of the year the temperature near sea level ranges between sixty-five and eighty-five degrees Fahrenheit; until about a dozen years ago a temperature of ninety degrees had not been recorded in Honolulu. Since then, for one reason or another—some people blame the high-rise buildings, the increase in paved areas, and the automobiles—temperatures of 90 degrees or higher have been recorded frequently during the summer.

Unlike the tropical areas near Asia, Hawaii does not have a regular rainy season, although the six months beginning in October have a higher average rainfall than the other six. Actually the rainfall varies much more from place to place than it does from month to month. As the trade winds lift the moisture-laden Pacific air up over the mountains of these high islands, the air cools and moisture precipitates, sometimes in unbelievable quantities. On Oahu, the Waikiki resort area has an average annual rainfall of only about twenty inches, which puts it close to the desert classification; about four miles away, at the back of Manoa Valley, the rainfall is over a hundred inches per year. The fact that rain precipitating above the mountains may be blown quite a distance before it lands gives rise to the phenomenon of "liquid sunshine," rain sprinkling out of a blue sky. The rain and sun combine to provide Hawaii's many rainbows.

A less decorative but equally attractive aspect of Hawaii is its program for education: a large, centrally administered school system which is unique among the fifty states, as well as a number of excellent private institutions. Punahou School, founded by early Protestant missionaries, has been in operation since 1841 and during the Gold Rush days drew students from California. The Kamehameha Schools, drawing income from a vast estate left by Bernice Pauahi Bishop, have provided private schooling for children of Hawaiian ancestry since 1887. Mid-Pacific Institute, another fine private school, is only a few years younger. Iolani School, an Episcopal school for boys, lists among its alumni Sun Yat-sen.

At the college level the most prominent institutions are Chaminade College (Catholic, 1955), the Church College of Hawaii (Mormon, 1955), the new Hawaii Loa College (Episcopal, Methodist, Presbyterian, and United Church of Christ, 1967), and the state institution, the University of Hawaii (1907). The University of Hawaii also has a four-year branch at Hilo, on the Big Island, and has established a number of community colleges on Oahu and the other islands. The main campus, in Manoa Valley, Honolulu, had an enrollment of 23,000 in the fall of 1971.

One of the most striking features of Hawaii today is the multiracial background of its people. The whole subject of what constitutes a race, or even whether or not such a thing as a "pure race" exists, has been undergoing much reevaluation by anthropologists in recent years. In Hawaii the subject is further confused by the increasing number of interracial marriages. In the middle 1960's it was estimated that over one-fourth of the population of Oahu was of mixed blood, and forty percent of the marriages today involve persons of different ethnic backgrounds, often partners who are themselves racially mixed.

In 1950, the last time that the U.S. Bureau of the Census attempted to determine racial categories in Hawaii, it found that 36.9 percent of the population was of Japanese ancestry, 23.0 Caucasian, 17.2 Hawaiian or part Hawaiian, 12.2 Filipino, 6.5 Chinese, and 4.2 "others," including Puerto Rican, Korean, Samoan, and Negro. The make-up today—if it could be determined—would show a great increase in the Caucasian and Filipino populations, principally through migration; since 1966 an annual average of 40,000 new residents has moved to the state. Caucasians are now for the first time probably the largest single group. The number of Negroes and Samoans, while not large in the overall picture, has also increased. It is expected that new immigration rules will bring many more future citizens from Asiatic countries than could come under the old racially restricted quotas.

The multiracial citizenry gives Hawaii a unique flavor which is shown not only in the people's faces but also in the foods they eat and the language they use. Where else can you find sliced raw fish (Japanese), *kim chee* (Korean), Portuguese sweet bread, and *laulaus* (Hawaiian steamed pork, fish, and taro leaves) on sale at every supermarket, along with dozens of other equally exotic items? Where else can you also attend in July and August a number of festive outdoor *bon* dances (Japanese) honoring the dead? Where else will you find *kamaaina* (old-time resident), *malihini* (newcomer), *haole* (Caucasian), *makai* (toward the sea), and dozens of other Hawaiian words part of the functional vocabulary of English-speaking people? Of course, some Hawaiian words have become absorbed into general English and can be found in your dictionary: *ukulele, lanai, aloha, muumuu,* and two words to describe types of lava—*aa* and *pahoehoe.*

Beyond this there is "pidgin English," a structurally simplified, somewhat awkward, but often expressive jargon which grew up in the early days in an attempt to establish communication between diverse peoples who had no common language. It comes in many varieties and degrees, some of them quite localized. Its influence is the despair of the purist English teacher, and yet command of it establishes a kind of bond between local people: some time is required for an outsider to handle it without sounding ridiculous. It is often tersely expressive: "Cool haid main t'ing" has calmed down many a hothead; "was'e time" is a succinct descriptive term for a person, book, or game you have no use for. And "da kine" is an all-purpose expression used either as adjective or indefinite pronoun. "You get da kine?" Or, "Wheah da kine feesh?"

Hawaii's racial situation today is not a paradise on earth. Some prejudice can be noted even between subgroups of people an outsider might consider as originally being of the same racial or even national background. But possibly nowhere else on earth do the different races in general get along so well—perhaps, as has been suggested, because for nearly eighty years everybody in the islands has been a member of a minority. The increasing number of interracial marriages makes it seem that the people of Hawaii are in the process of creating a fusion of races not quite like any other on earth. And yet one hopes that all the sense of diverse bloods and all the pride and knowledge of an individual's backgrounds will not be obliterated.

OAHU

The first stop most visitors from the mainland U.S.A. make in Hawaii is at the island of Oahu, where the port and airport of Honolulu are. From either sea or air, Oahu's rugged character is evident. A lighthouse sits on top of a cliff at Makapuu Point, the easternmost tip of the island, 400 feet above the water. Then following a stretch of beach the sea dashes against several miles of steep, rocky coastline. Near the ocean the land looks dry and brown, but back in the hills it grows greener. The large ancient volcanoes which originally created the island have long ago been eroded into steep ridges and deep valleys, but along the coast some clearly volcanic outlines from what a geologist would call "recent" eruptions—within the last 33,000 to 300,000 years —can be seen. Koko Crater projects a large extinct cone 1,200 feet into the air; Koko Head, 640 feet high, lies like a huge whale at the water's edge; between them the seaward side of yet another crater has fallen into the sea, creating charming semicircular Hanauma Bay, now a city park.

Ahead lies Oahu's most famous landmark, Diamond Head, a large hollow cone over a mile across at its base, a half mile across at its top, and 760 feet high at its seaward peak. From sea level it looks just like another steep ridge; its crater shape can be seen from the air or from some of the heights which rise behind it or

Aerial view of Diamond Head shows peak rising to seven hundred sixty feet and crater containing government installations.

by entering its hollow through a tunnel in its side. Known as Leahi to the Hawaiians because its shape is that of the brow of the *ahi* tuna, it was called Diamond Head when some early British sailors picked up sparkling stones at its base and thought they had found diamonds.

Beyond Diamond Head lies Waikiki, and still further on is downtown Honolulu. Honolulu is a large modern American city, ranking for about the last twenty years among the fifty largest (almost the size of Miami, Tulsa, and Omaha, according to the 1970 census), with a resident population of nearly 325,-000. But politically the City and County of Honolulu, comprising the entire 600-square-mile island, is one unit with a single city council, mayor, tax structure, and police force. Its 1970 population was over 630,000, which would rank it above Boston, St. Louis, and New Orleans among the top two dozen cities in the country.

Waikiki is a cluster of towering hotels, some 250 feet high, with many more still a-building. Where Waikiki had 5,300 hotel rooms in early 1960, it had 19,300 in 1971. The construction crane, rather than Diamond Head, seems to have become the symbol of Honolulu, as familiar views of the hills and sea give way to walls of concrete. The famous 196-foot Aloha Tower near the harbor is now dwarfed by some of the larger buildings of downtown Honolulu.

Honolulu is not only the political but also the industrial and financial capital of the fiftieth state. Here are the centers of the two big agricultural industries, sugar and pineapple (the latter clearly symbolized by "the world's largest pineapple," a pineapple-shaped water tower which stands above the Dole cannery). Within walking distance of the waterfront are the centers and symbols of both old and new Hawaii. Beyond the tall commercial buildings stands the handsomely gingerbready Iolani Palace, built in 1882, containing the only throne room under the

The world's largest pineapple serves as the Dole cannery's water tower.

American flag. Across the street is a gold and brown statue of the first king of all Hawaii, Kamehameha I (c. 1758–1819). On the Palace grounds is also Iolani Barracks, military center of the former monarchy, looking like a toy-soldier fortification. Behind the Palace a whole block is occupied by the new State Capitol, its soaring supports like stylized coconut trees. It emerges, island-like, from surrounding pools and has an open top like a volcanic crater.

Across Beretania Street (named for Britain) from the new Capitol is Washington Place, once the home of Hawaii's last monarch, Queen Liliuokalani. It is now the official residence of the governor of Hawaii. Not far from the palace rises the clock tower of Kawaiahao Church, erected in 1842 on a site which had been used for Christian worship since 1821. In the front yard of

Iolani Palace contains the only throne room in the United States.

the church is the tomb of one of the last Hawaiian kings, and in an adjacent area stand buildings used as dwellings and as a printing house by Protestant missionaries a century and a half ago. The cathedrals of the Catholic and Episcopal churches are also within half a mile of Aloha Tower. Behind the city rises 500-foot Punchbowl Crater, site of the National Cemetery of the Pacific.

Honolulu today has most of the attractions and many of the disadvantages one might expect to find in a large city. It has fine residential districts, and slums, too. At certain times of day colossal traffic jams occur. They might be considerably reduced if people used the bus system instead of their own cars, but few do. The Ala Moana Shopping Center, an extremely well-designed facility, is perhaps the biggest in the world and includes the largest Sears store anywhere!

In 1966 the Washington International Arts letter reported—after conducting a computerized evaluation of certain cultural criteria—that Hawaii seemed to be the most cultured state in the union. What has Honolulu to offer culturally? There are a professional symphony orchestra, a chamber music society, a gem of an Academy of Arts (featuring an excellent collection of Oriental art and a fine representation of Western art), an annual opera festival, and a great variety of theatre. Also, the Bishop Museum, the Polynesian Cultural Center, and the Ulu Mau Village specialize in Pacific culture. The Foster Gardens, a small but interesting collection of tropical trees and plants, lie within walking distance of downtown Honolulu. In Waikiki are a well-kept zoo and an aquarium with a spectacular display of reef fish.

Oahu is also a military center. The famous naval base at Pearl Harbor stands on a large three-branched inlet in the low south coast of the island; Camp H. M. Smith (Marines) is the center of command for all Pacific military forces; Fort Shafter is Army headquarters for the Pacific. Barber's Point Naval Air Station, Kaneohe Marine Corps Air Station, Hickam Field, a Coast Guard Station, and Schofield Barracks are other important military sites on Oahu. Also on the island are communications stations, ammunition storage, a huge underground fuel reservoir, and defensive missile sites. The total number of military personnel stationed ashore in Hawaii has averaged well over fifty thousand for the last ten years.

Oahu's air bases, including several now inactive, and naval vessels and facilities at Pearl Harbor suffered the major destruction from Japan's sneak attack by carrier planes shortly after dawn on December 7, 1941. Caught on the ground or in hangars, the great majority of American planes were destroyed or put out of action before they could rise to the defense. All seven battleships tied up in "Battleship Row" in Pearl Harbor were hit by bombs and torpedoes; several of the vessels ended up on the bottom. The greatest losses were to the *Oklahoma*, which capsized, and the *Arizona*, which exploded violently and sank when a bomb touched off her magazine. For several days after the attack, survivors trapped in the hull of the *Oklahoma* were rescued by workmen cutting through her massive bottom. More than twenty-three hundred men of the U. S. Navy, Marines, and Army lost their lives, and over eleven hundred were wounded.

Civilian areas of Oahu received comparatively little damage from the Japanese that day; fewer than sixty civilians were killed. The thoroughly trained attackers used their bombs and ammunition on military targets; most of the damage in Honolulu and other civilian areas was caused by falling American anti-aircraft projectiles and shrapnel. Losses to the Japanese attacking force were unbelievably light; twenty-nine planes failed to return to their carriers, and the carriers themselves were not located.

The *U. S. S. Arizona* and the old *Utah* have never been raised from their Pearl Harbor graves. Protected against enemy shells (but not bombs or torpedoes) by a foot or two of steel armor, they still lie under the calm water of Pearl Harbor, the tombs of the men that died in them—1,100 men in the *Arizona* and 54 in the *Utah*.

One can easily visit the *Arizona* Memorial, perhaps our nation's most impressive military shrine, on a cruise boat from Honolulu or on a Navy boat which leaves from a Pearl Harbor pier. The superstructure of the *Arizona*, all that remained above water December 7, was removed during the war years; the mas-

Beside the graceful *Arizona* Memorial, a few portions of the sunken hulk still break the surface of Pearl Harbor.

sive hulk lies underwater. Upon it has been constructed a beautiful concrete structure, combining strong vertical lines and graceful curves, partly open to Hawaii's sun and trade winds. On the walls is an alphabetical list of the *Arizona* men who died. In the water below can be seen the hull, covered now with inches of seaweed and barnacles. From time to time oil still seeps up from the battered ship, even after more than thirty years.

Oahu has good beaches along much of its coastline, although some of them are dangerous for inexperienced swimmers. Waikiki Beach, which sometimes disappoints newcomers by being smaller and more crowded than they expected, lies on the lee side of Oahu and is one of the safer ones. Early in the century Waikiki was the favorite spot for surfers. In recent years, with new varieties of boards and improved techniques, surfers are riding bigger waves at Makaha Beach and at some of the "dan-

Surfing on the waves off Oahu is not easy—but it's fun.

gerous" beaches along the North Shore; both locations have
been sites of international competitions.

The beaches of Hawaii, whose sand is composed largely of
worn bits of shells of sea animals, have taken many thousands
of years to form. A serious threat to several of Oahu's beaches
arose when people who assumed that it would be replaced naturally in a year or two took quantities of sand for concrete. Strict
regulations, the use of "sand" manufactured from rocks, and the
importation of beach sand from Molokai have coped with this
threat.

Hawaii's natural resources, besides the Pacific Ocean and its
climate, are its land and its fresh water. There is no likelihood
of oil deposits, and iron and aluminum, present in large
amounts, are in forms that have not proved commercially usable. Agriculture, from the start the base of Hawaii's livelihood,
developed with sugar in the nineteenth century and pineapple
in the twentieth.

Over one-third of the state's prime agricultural land is on Oahu, although originally much of it was unproductive for lack of a steady supply of water. The heavy rainfall in the mountains normally either sinks into the porous soil or runs off rapidly to the ocean; there are no rivers to serve as dependable water sources or lakes to act as reservoirs. However, it was discovered that nature had provided two kinds of natural underground fresh-water reservoirs: a tremendous body or "lens" of artesian water, first drilled into in 1879, underlies much of southern Oahu, and at higher elevations great pockets of porous, water-filled rock lie trapped between walls of harder rock. The latter sources have been tapped by tunnels.

Although Oahu has a large supply of water, there is none to spare. Sugarcane is a thirsty crop, taking two tons of water to produce a pound of sugar, and the water needs of Oahu's swelling population and growing industries are increasing rapidly. The water level in the artesian basin has dropped seventeen feet in ninety years, and for every foot it drops at the top, salt water encroaches forty feet from below. Development of additional water sources and conservation of the old are continually being carried out.

Agriculture has been engaging in an increasingly serious competition with housing, business, industry, and in some instances the military, for the use of Oahu's limited land. Oahu had six sugar plantations in the 1930's; today there are two. Driving from Pearl Harbor northward in the fertile region between the two ranges one passes through sugarcane fields at the lower levels and pineapple fields higher up. The demands of housing, however, are gnawing away at this fertile belt. Near the town of Waipahu several large tracts of sugar land have been turned into subdivisions, and elsewhere a former pineapple area is being converted into a new small city which will eventually hold 25,000 people. Cultivation on less desirable acreage both on Oahu and on other islands has in part made up for this loss of prime agricultural land.

Hawaii's raw sugar production has averaged about 1.2 million tons annually in recent years. Mark Twain was impressed by the technology of Hawaii's sugar industry, and Hawaii continues to lead the world in efficiency of production by continual application of scientific research in plant breeding, plant diseases, pest control, and improved methods of cultivation and sugar extraction. The high average yield of ten tons of sugar per acre is in part also the result of the fact that cane in Hawaii grows two years before harvest, as opposed to one year in cane-growing areas such as Louisiana.

A cane field is burned before harvest to destroy leaves and trash, leaving the juice-filled stalks unharmed. The cane is mechanically harvested, trucked to the mill, cleaned, and its juice extracted. Evaporation and other processes produce raw sugar, which is hauled in huge bulk trucks to a loading plant and put aboard bulk freighters for transportation to mainland refineries, where it is converted into the product you find on your table. Only a small amount of sugar for local use receives its final

Working in a sugarcane field, woman replants bare spots for second-growth; men with knapsack sprayers kill weeds among young cane.

refining at one plant in Hawaii. Mechanization has reduced the total labor needs in the industry to under twelve thousand—less than a third of the force needed earlier in the century. Correspondingly, through union bargaining average wages have risen steadily, giving the Hawaii field worker hourly wages about twice those of the average field worker in other sugar-producing states.

Two big canneries in Honolulu process most of Hawaii's pineapple. To them the "pines" are brought in huge bins by truck from Oahu fields and by barge from the islands of Molokai and Lanai. An ingenious machine removes the skin (later converted into cattle feed) and core, but further trimming and filling of cans is done by a large crew of white-gowned female workers. Since the big pineapple harvest comes in the summer months, cannery and field work provide many thousands of seasonal jobs for students.

Perhaps you have wondered how a pineapple is planted, since it is normally a seedless fruit. The top which is cut off a fruit can be allowed to dry for some days and then, when stuck into the soil, will eventually send forth roots and develop into a new plant—try it. Other portions of the plant, called slips, will develop similarly. Tops or slips are planted through holes poked in a long strip of polyethylene film laid on the field. The film serves as a mulch, providing warmth, conserving moisture, and protecting the young plant from the competition of weeds.

Hawaii's pineapple industry, while at present still growing slightly in dollar value, is beginning to receive strong competition from foreign regions with cheaper labor, notably Taiwan and the Philippines. Once Hawaii produced by far the majority of the world's canned pineapple, but today it produces forty percent.

Oahu is also the site of "diversified agriculture," the production of fruit, vegetables, eggs, poultry, pork, beef, and milk for the local market. Yet Oahu (and Hawaii as a whole) imports more of most items than it produces. As time goes by Oahu will become more dependent on the neighboring islands for locally grown items.

With the greatest concentration of Hawaii's population, Oahu is also Hawaii's center for other industries. In 1970, completed construction of hotels, residences, and other public and private projects amounted to a record $721 million on Oahu alone, employing among other materials the output of two cement manufacturing plants. Besides the usual food and drink plants, making such items as bread, hot dogs, soft drinks, and beer, Honolulu has a tuna cannery and a number of small plants producing Oriental and Hawaiian foods. A can company manufactures the empty containers for Honolulu's canneries. The garment industry, specializing in Hawaiian sportswear for residents and tourists, has been very successful. Without attempting to list all of Honolulu's manufacturing industries, with products ranging from perfumes to fertilizers, we might merely note that as the population grows, it often becomes profitable to establish a plant to manufacture some product which previously has been imported ready-made.

A large part of Oahu—and of Hawaii's other islands as well —particularly at the higher elevations, is in forest reserve. A good deal of this land is too steep or is otherwise unsuitable for either agriculture, industry, or housing; much of it is designated "closed watershed" in order to conserve the natural resource of rainfall. Many areas have been planted with introduced trees: eucalyptus from Australia, silk oak, and a variety of conifers. They often grow better in Hawaii's climate than they did in their native habitat because they tend to put forth growth over more months of the year. A controlled forestry program, with a proper balance between lumbering and conservation, might provide the state with a sizeable portion of its lumber, most of which is now imported.

One unusual export from Hawaii, which has been increasing from a small beginning, is young Norfolk Island Pine trees during the Christmas season. Extremely attractive and symmetrical, and not apt to shed needles, these trees draw premium prices on the mainland for use in Yuletide displays. When a tree has been cut, the stump will produce a new tree of the same size in a few years, making steady cropping possible. For their own use, most people in Hawaii continue to use the less expensive Christmas trees brought in by the shipload from the Northwest.

Many of Hawaii's mountain areas are also used by the military for training in jungle warfare and by civilians for recreation. Those who like hunting can find a variety of introduced game: pheasants, wild pigs, goats, deer, and even wild cattle. Hiking along the numerous established trails which provide spectacular views of mountains, valleys, and the ocean is a popular recreation. It is possible, within three miles of the crowded Waikiki district, to be on a forest trail, away from buildings and traffic. Hawaii has no poisonous snakes, but the alluring green mountains are dangerous for those who wander off the trails. Every year dozens of people, not believing that one can get lost on a little island, are plucked from steep ridges or pulled from tangled thickets by helicopters and specially trained rescue squads; less fortunate ones have lost their lives.

Of course, one does not have to get out on a trail to look at Oahu's beauty. A drive along the northeast, or windward, side of the island, on the low-lying region between the Koolau moun-

From the Koolau Range, the *pali*, or cliffs, drop steeply in folds for many hundreds of feet.

tains and the sea, provides a view of miles of the erosion-produced *pali,* or cliffs, where the Koolaus drop steeply from their summits in folds like a green curtain. One low notch (only 1,186 feet above sea level) is the famous Nuuanu Pali, at the head of Nuuanu Valley, which runs down on the leeward side of the island toward Honolulu harbor. When King Kamehameha the conqueror invaded Oahu in 1795, he drove a number of the Oahu defenders up this valley in a running battle which ended when many of the losing army leaped or were pushed from the Pali to their death. The Pali Lookout at the site of this event provides an excellent view of much of windward Oahu. Because the trade winds funnel through this notch in the mountains it also provides surprisingly strong winds on even an average day. On windier days it is possible to lean at an unbelievable angle against the wind, and small cars have been overturned by especially strong gusts. Not far away, at the "Upside Down Falls," this same wind sometimes blows a group of small waterfalls upward from the edge of their cliff.

KAUAI

Interisland travel in Hawaii today across the often rough channels is by airplane, either on the jet fleets of the two scheduled airlines (which have the world's best safety record) or on the planes of several nonscheduled carriers. Kauai is about a hundred miles to the northwest of Oahu, little more than twenty minutes by jet. Coming in to land at the Lihue airport, laid out on level land among sugarcane fields, visitors fly over one of Kauai's two principal harbors, the port of Nawiliwili.

Kauai is the fourth largest island in the state, both in area (551 square miles) and population. Although its 29,500 people are fewer than the 35,000 of thirty years ago, it is believed that the number will grow in the future. Recently, within a five-year period, the Kauai tourist industry quadrupled. However, sugar, with eight plantations supplying one-fifth of the state's crop, was still the island's major source of income in 1970. The larger Kauai towns—and all are under five thousand in population—started as plantation communities and still show their origin. Beef cattle are also raised on this island, and pineapple is grown, although the area devoted to this crop has decreased in recent years.

Originally formed from a single huge volcano, since carved upon by erosion, Kauai today is nearly circular, thirty-two miles in diameter. Low-lying lands suitable for agriculture are found along about two-thirds of its coastline, extending inland for as much as six or seven miles in some places. In the center of Kauai is mile-high Mount Waialeale, whose summit is among the less frequently visited wonders of the world. Indeed, much of the time it isn't even visible, for according to the National Geographic Society it is the wettest spot on earth; the average annual rainfall is over 470 inches! An event of minor local importance used to be the annual expedition up Waialeale's usually sodden sides to read and empty the rain guage; in some years the figures were not accurate because it had overflowed. Today, records are kept by automatic instruments, and the recording station can be reached—when weather permits—by helicopter.

The heavy rainfall has created a large swampy area near the island's summit, the home of rare forms of plant and bird life, and is responsible for the numerous waterfalls and the stream-carved valleys which extend to the sea. Another result is the lush greenery which covers most of the island and gives it its nickname, "The Garden Island."

One cannot make a complete circuit of Kauai by road. On the drive from Lihue along the east and north sides of the island, the road comes to an abrupt end at Haena, at the beginning of the Napali (Cliffs) Coast, which extends along the island's northwest side. Here great cliffs drop hundreds or even several thousands of feet into the Pacific. Punctuating this expanse of cliff are a number of valleys, the larger ones formerly inhabited. No families have lived in them regularly since early in this century; they are too inaccessible.

At the end of the road, it is interesting to hike for a few miles along a trail that leads part of the way along the coast, skirting the tops of cliffs, winding into minor indentations, and zigzagging down into and up out of the deeper valleys. Used by Hawaiians for centuries when the coast was populated, it is called the "Seven Mile Trail," but each mile seems like two. At the start, a steep pull up leads to the brink of a cliff from which one can get a breathtaking view of the expanse of the coast with the ocean beating at its base. Several miles farther on is the first large valley, once the site of a coffee plantation.

Good camping and hiking equipment are needed if one wants to go on to the end of the trail at Kalalau Valley, a large and beautiful valley surrounded by steep cliffs which rise to 4,000 feet at its head. Once the home of hundreds of Hawaiians, this valley is now visited by goat hunters and campers. In recent years it has for periods had a resident hermit, and it has not been overlooked by nature-loving hippies. It has a nice sandy beach at its mouth, and inland one can find old house sites and terraces once used for taro growing. Those who do not wish to lug their equipment over the tortuous trail can get to Kalalau by boat in good weather. For those with enough money to pay for the fare, a helicopter provides an even easier and faster means of getting to this and to other isolated valleys (some of which are entirely inaccessible by land) along the coast.

The road from Haena to Lihue passes a series of three caves, two of them containing fresh-water pools, occasionally visited by those who like swimming in a spooky atmosphere. Farther on, the beautiful beach at Lumahai and nearby Hanalei Bay have both been used as moving picture settings.

Wailua River, five miles north of Lihue, fed by water from Mount Waialeale, is the most navigable river in the state, though a mainlander might call it a creek. A resort area is being developed near its mouth, and boat rides can be taken along its lower course. On its banks are the remains of several old Hawaiian *heiaus*, or temples, and other sites of prehistoric significance. A large tropical garden displaying a wide variety of Hawaiian trees and flowers has been laid out along one stretch of the river.

To see the attractions of the other half of Kauai, one must proceed through Lihue and go clockwise around the south side of the island. A branch road toward the ocean leads to Koloa, where stand the ruins of the first sugar mill in Hawaii (1835). The shore area near Koloa contains several tourist hotels, particularly at Poipu Beach, and the Spouting Horn, a blowhole where the ocean shoots up through an opening in the rock beside the water with moaning sound effects.

Port Allen, the other principal port, is seventeen miles from Lihue; another eight miles of highway through cane lands leads to Waimea, a small town near the mouth of the Waimea River. On the east bank of the river, not far from the road, stands a fort built by the Russians in 1817, when Russia seemed about to establish control over not only Hawaii but also a good bit of the western coast of North America from San Francisco Bay northward.

Along the coast a dozen miles beyond Waimea are "Barking Sands," so called because the granular structure of the sand creates a rather canine sound when two handfuls of it are tossed together forcibly. During the war an air base was constructed there, and the site is now part of a military installation which includes an antisubmarine test range extending miles out to sea. The real barking sands may be all covered over with paving now.

A Pacific wonder is the Waimea Canyon. Somehow, nobody expects to find on such a small island as Kauai a midocean Grand Canyon over half a mile deep. But there it is, another result of the tremendous amount of rain that falls in Kauai's uplands. Many people think Waimea is actually more beautiful than the Grand Canyon, with more variety in the color of its sides—green growth and bright red soil contrasting with the duller shades of rock. From lookout points along the road visitors look down into the awesome depths to the tiny ribbon of water below and into the reaches of branch canyons on the far side.

Long-tailed white tropic birds, which nest in the canyon's

sides, circle below; occasionally one catches a glimpse of a wild goat, surely bent on suicide, making his way along a narrow ledge on the side of a 2,000-foot dropoff. Here and there the canyon is punctuated by a tall pinnacle of harder rock which somehow resisted the erosion of the stream that swept around it. (Waimea Canyon is actually not Kauai's deepest valley; three large valleys on the north side of the island are even deeper but are rarely seen except from the air.)

At an elevation of 3,500 to 4,000 feet is the Kokee area. Mostly forest reserve and in part a state park with cabins, camping facilities, and a small museum, Kokee has also been for years the site of many vacation lodges owned by Kauai residents. The first necessity for a Kokee cabin is a fireplace, for at this elevation the temperature at night can drop to the fifties in any month of the year and may even reach the thirties in cold weather.

Many of Hawaii's mountain tops are used today for scientific purposes of one sort or another. At Kokee, a tracking station of critical importance in America's space program has been built, part of the network used to maintain voice and instrument communications between our spacecraft and earth. In January of 1969 the trackers on duty had an unusual weather experience: over thirty-four inches of rain fell in one twenty-four-hour period. It must have been like living under a waterfall.

A few miles past the Kokee Park center the road ends at a magnificent lookout over Kalalau Valley. Below the 4,000-foot elevation, clouds drift into the valley and swirl upward; on many days the lookout is completely cloud-wrapped. A steep buttressed ridge sticks out from the uplands, forming the far side of the valley until it plunges to the ocean. Far below a razor-sharp spur, on which binoculars reveal several inevitable goats nonchalantly promenading, is probably a mere two or three thousand feet above the valley's floor. But it takes more than binoculars to see Kalalau as it once was, a thriving, populated, self-sufficient Hawaiian valley.

From the road back down to sea level, another island is visible to the southwest across a seventeen-mile channel. This is Niihau the remote, for over a hundred years the private property of the

Robinson family of Kauai and home of nearly three hundred Hawaiians. Lying on the lee side of Kauai and only 1,281 feet above sea level at its highest point, Niihau lacks Kauai's abundant rainfall. Sheep and cattle in limited numbers are raised on the seventy-two-square-mile island, and honey is produced.

The Robinsons have carefully preserved the Hawaiian way of life on their island ranch. All but three of the residents are of Hawaiian blood, two-thirds of them pure Hawaiian. Outsiders are not welcome, unless on business. The people live in frame houses, not grass shacks, but they have no central power system and are dependent for food staples on a Robinson-owned supply boat. The island has no barrooms and no police, and on Sunday the Christian church is regularly attended. Niihau children attend a public school up to the eighth grade; the few who desire further education must seek it on another island. In school, the lessons are in English, but among themselves the islanders use the musical Hawaiian language. Two Hawaiian crafts from Niihau which are prized by collectors are unbelievably fine mats woven from a sort of grass, and delicate shell leis made from hundreds of tiny shells found on the beaches.

The Hawaiian chain of islands, resulting from volcanic activity along a huge crack in the floor of the Pacific, does not stop at Niihau. To the northwest for a thousand miles more along this line extend the Leeward (or Northwestern) Islands of the chain, the tops of a great underwater mountain range. Some of them barely rise above sea level; others have been worn down to small pinnacles or shoals. Nihoa, 250 miles from Honolulu, and Necker, 150 miles farther away, are especially interesting since they bear evidence that ancient Hawaiians established small settlements and temples there and then abandoned them centuries before Hawaii was visited by Europeans.

The Leeward Islands today are all considered uninhabitable, although at times shipwrecked sailors have managed to survive on them while awaiting rescue. On two of them, however, are installations which are regularly supplied from the outside. On French Frigate Shoals, where a small airstrip has been created on a speck of an atoll, about twenty Coast Guardsmen operate a LORAN station. Midway Island, over 1,300 miles from Honolulu near the end of the chain, is a naval reservation where several thousand people live. It has a good airfield, formerly a regular refueling stop for transpacific planes.

But for the most part the Leeward Islands are a wildlife refuge inhabited by hundreds of thousands of sea birds—albatrosses, terns, frigate birds, boobies, noddy terns, sooty terns, tropic

A loran station at French Frigate Shoals, a lonely island five hundred fifty miles northwest of Honolulu, is run by the United States Coast Guard.

birds—as well as turtles and the rare Hawaiian monk seal. For man, "No Trespassing" signs are posted.

MOLOKAI

Oahu's nearest neighbor, Molokai, "The Friendly Island," lies across Kaiwi channel, a twenty-five mile stretch of usually turbulent water where outrigger-canoe crews test their stamina in an annual island-to-island race. The crossing has even been tried by swimmers, twice successfully. Molokai's outline is like that of a fish thirty-seven miles long and ten miles wide, its tail pointing west toward Oahu. A fin projecting from the north side is the peninsula of Kalaupapa. Much of the western end of the island is an elevated plain; in the eastern end mountains rise to nearly five thousand feet. The island's principal port and town, Kaunakakai, is midway along the southern coast.

Molokai originally supported a large number of Hawaiians, who built many artificial enclosures in the shallow waters along the south shore for the raising of food fish. The lands were not suitable for sugar, however, and although ranching was established many people moved away to more prosperous islands. In seventy-five years the population dropped from six thousand to barely one thousand. When pineapple production was started in the 1920's the population grew rapidly for a while. In the same decade the creation of forty-acre homesteads on Molokai, open to people of at least half Hawaiian blood, induced a number of Hawaiian families to reoccupy parts of the island.

Molokai did not change greatly from the 1930's to the 1960's, but Molokai's period of dormancy is probably now over. Within the next decade its face should change greatly. Lack of water had limited agricultural production on the island's western plain, including the homestead area, while at the same time the heavy rainfall at the island's high east end ran off northward through steep valleys to the sea. A water-development project including a five-mile-long tunnel has tapped one of these valleys and led its water westward; an artificial, rubber-lined earth reservoir holding 1.4 billion gallons will ensure a stable year-round supply. Future tunnels and facilities are on the drawing boards. The water will irrigate acres devoted to diversified agriculture—corn, tomatoes, and potatoes—as well as pineapples.

A recently introduced industry is growing hybridized seed corn. Hybridization requires a number of plant generations to develop a new strain, and on the mainland a plant breeder can get only one generation per year. In Hawaii's year-round summer about two generations per year are possible. Perhaps "Developed in Hawaii" will one day appear on the bags of the seed used for the best Iowa corn!

Tourists, who began coming to Molokai's one resort hotel in the 1960's, will be arriving in greater numbers as more facilities are built. The west shore of the island has magnificent beaches, and the owners are proceeding with plans to convert this rarely visited end of the island into a resort, vacation, and residential development. It has even been predicted that transportation advances could turn western Molokai into a suburb of Honolulu.

A flight along the north coast of Molokai reveals cliffs that drop to the sea—a few hundred feet high at the western end and three thousand or more feet at the mountainous east end. As on the Napali Coast of Kauai, several steep valleys, formerly inhabited and inaccessible except by sea, penetrate inland. At the base of 2,000-foot cliffs projecting two miles into the ocean is low-lying Makanalua Peninsula (often called Kalaupapa), formed by the eruption of a crater at its center. This is the site of the historic "leper settlement" of Molokai.

Leprosy, sometimes called Hansen's Disease, was one of the many foreign diseases to which Polynesians seemed to have a low natural immunity. Presumably introduced to the islands around 1830 from Asia and locally called "the Chinese Disease," leprosy spread rapidly, and victims of the disease were isolated, since there was no known cure. In 1865 an isolation hospital was opened in Honolulu; the next year Kalawao, a settlement on the Molokai peninsula, was opened for confirmed chronic cases. Kalaupapa, a town near by, was developed later. During the rest of the century hundreds of victims of the disease were sent to the settlement, most of them doomed to increasing disfigurement, often severe crippling, and eventual death. Many relatives, wives, husbands, and friends voluntarily exiled themselves to tend the sufferers.

Into this settlement of disease and human decay also came a number of church workers. The most famous was a Roman Catholic priest from Belgium, Father Damien. Father Damien lived and worked among the leprosy patients from 1873 to 1889, eventually contracting leprosy himself and dying of the disease. Damien's accomplishments have been the subject of several books, and his memory is more deeply revered with the passing years. Steps have been taken toward his beatification, and possibly one day he will be made a saint by the Catholic church. Upon admission to statehood Hawaii was given the privilege, like all states, of putting statues of two of her outstanding historical figures in the Capitol at Washington. The two chosen were King Kamehameha and the leper priest.

Although a few patients naturally overcame the disease, nothing seemed to cure leprosy. The victims were in a way fortunate: the disease numbed the nerves that transmit pain. But that did not prolong the lives of those whose bodies were unable to resist it. For some years chaulmoogra oil, obtained from the seeds of a tree, was used as a treatment, but nobody is sure whether or not it helped. Finally, in the 1940's and following years, drugs were developed which have been remarkably successful in leprosy treatment.

Actually, leprosy, although contagious, is one of the least contagious diseases, less so than tuberculosis or even the common cold. Very few people are susceptible to it, and modern drugs can usually stop it in a relatively short period of time. Hawaii's laws of strict isolation may be modified to allow people who have contracted the disease to move about in society after a shorter hospitalization, when tests have proven that treatment has halted the bacteria. Today new patients undergo treatment at a special 100-bed hospital on Oahu and usually never see Molokai.

But the Molokai settlement still exists. The old village of Kalawao shows little more than its foundation stones, but the village of Kalaupapa stands. Of the 172 residents in 1970, fewer than 125 were patients; the others were staff and relatives of patients. Some of the patients have been there for years and do not wish, either because of their physical condition or their fear of prejudice in employment or their lack of employable skills, to return to the "outside world." New patients also may, at their own request, commit themselves to Kalaupapa for life. Here they will receive free lodging, medical care, food, and a small allowance, and may earn additional money, if able.

In the old days the only ways to get to Kalaupapa were by boat, in good weather, or by a trail which winds its way down the 2,000-foot cliff. A stable of mules was kept to transport officials and necessary goods down the hazardous path. Father Damien, who did not limit his ministration to the peninsula, must have gone up and down this trail countless times, for he established a number of churches, some of which still stand, elsewhere on Molokai. Today one can drive from Kaunakakai to the top of the trail and look at the peninsula far below; with permission the sturdy may take the hike down and back. A small, partially-paved runway now provides an easier access by light plane, and since the advent of new drugs, sightseeing visitors are allowed. Licensed tour drivers, none of whom can be active patients, provide tours of the village or, over bumpy roads, of other parts of the peninsula. Between the airstrip and the town lies a large cemetery. Within the town, patients who need regular care live in larger buildings; others have neat, simple cottages of their own. Most of the automobiles are rather old—they don't wear out from mileage on this small peninsula. It takes a while before one realizes why the town has a strange atmosphere: there are no children, for they are thought to be more susceptible than adults to the disease.

From the southeast shore of Molokai, two islands loom across intervening channels. One is Lanai, sixth largest of the Hawaiian islands, little more than half the size of Molokai. Lanai was bought by the Dole Pineapple Company in the 1920's and today is a one-industry island; one-sixth of its area is devoted to pineapple. About three thousand people live there year-round, and additional workers come during the height of the season. The island has several fine beaches, but few visitors or accommodations for them. Fishing and hunting are good, however, and the island has a number of old Hawaiian historical sites.

MAUI

Maui, Hawaii's second largest island (728 square miles), is the big neighbor of Molokai and Lanai. It is shaped like a very lopsided figure eight, with a small western end and a large triangular eastern end connected by a wide, low-lying isthmus. Each end was once a volcano, the smaller eroding to form the West Maui Mountains, which are over a mile high, and the larger consisting of the single, 10,000-foot-high Haleakala. Maui's nickname, "The Valley Island," probably comes not from the many valleys which penetrate these two mountains but from the huge valley lying between them. Miles of cane grow in the lowlands sloping up from the isthmus. Maui's three plantations, one of which is the largest in America, produce nearly a quarter of Hawaii's sugar.

Kahului, Maui's chief port, is at the north side of Maui's neck; the Kahului airport is not far away. To the east Haleakala's massive dome rises impressively; in the other direction the city of Wailuku sits near the mouth of Iao Valley at the base of the rugged West Maui Mountains.

Kahului and Wailuku are growing toward one another in a succession of developments along the three-mile highway that

Iao Needle is highlight of the Iao Valley in Maui.

joins them. Wailuku is the center of government for Maui County, which comprises the islands of Maui, Lanai, and all of Molokai except Kalaupapa's peninsula. When Kamehameha conquered Maui in 1790, Iao Valley was the scene of a battle so fierce, it is said, that the bodies of the slain blocked the valley's wildly rushing stream. The battle was called Kepaniwai, "the damming of the waters"; Wailuku's name means "water of destruction." Iao is a beautiful green narrow gorge bordered by sheer towering mountains. One majestic pinnacle, Iao Needle, 2,250 feet high, dominates the valley floor.

There is no way through the West Maui Mountains, and only skilled mountaineers attempt the dangerous climb over them. To get to historic Lahaina, one must drive back down Iao Valley, across the isthmus, and west along a scenic coast. Across about fifteen miles of channel lies arid Kahoolawe, forty-five square miles in area, once the site of a ranching operation. For years now it has been abandoned but is used regularly and intensively for target practice by ships and planes of the United States fleet. People are forbidden to land because of the danger from unexploded bombs, shells, and missiles—and also because the Navy wants to be sure the island is clear when firing begins. Still farther along, Lanai is visible across another channel.

Lahaina is a sugar town, port, and the gateway to the Kaanapali Coast, an upsurging tourist region. In the first half of the nineteenth century it was one of the most important cities in Hawaii. Several of Hawaii's kings chose to spend a good deal of time there, and for some years Lahaina served as a sort of joint capital of the islands, along with Honolulu. Lahaina also became an early center for mission and educational work. Lahainaluna School, founded in 1831 and the oldest school west of the Rocky Mountains, is today a public high school for the district. Here missionaries established a printing press which turned out books in the Hawaiian language and Hawaii's first newspaper. Young Hawaiians with scholarly interests were encouraged to conduct research into Hawaiian history and customs, many of which were even then passing from memory.

Lahaina's use as a port for whalers was what really made the town jump in the old days. While Honolulu had a better harbor and repair facilities, the waters off Lahaina, sheltered by Maui, Lanai, and Molokai, provided a safe anchorage—"Lahaina Roads"—for a nearly unlimited number of vessels. In the fall and the spring the rugged, water-weary, recreation-hungry, and sometimes lawless whalers poured ashore, causing problems for missionaries and peace officers. In 1846, Lahaina's biggest year, 429 whaling ships came to port. In recent years an annual festival, the Lahaina Whaling Spree, has been held, a controlled revival of the old-time gaiety.

Mindful of Lahaina's history, Mauians have taken steps to preserve and restore the town's historic sites with private and government funds. The Restoration Foundation has restored the home of the Reverend Dwight Baldwin, a missionary who came to the islands in 1831 and conducted a mission for thirty-six years. In the future other buildings may be restored or authentically rebuilt. Two old buildings near the waterfront, the courthouse and the Pioneer Inn, give a nineteenth-century air to the heart of the town. If the planners of Lahaina can succeed in turning down the pleas of those who would change its dimensions by erecting high-rise buildings between the ocean and the mountains, it may become a living exhibit of Hawaiian history.

The three-masted bark *Carthaginian*, following its use as the missionary ship in the movie *Hawaii*, was converted into Lahaina's floating museum of the whaling days. It was unfortunately wrecked on a reef in 1972, and the Foundation is seeking a replacement.

A few miles beyond Lahaina lies an area which up to a few years ago had several wonderful unpopulated beaches, a good deal of sugar cane, and some pineapple fields. Today the portions near the ocean are undergoing extensive development into a major resort area, Kaanapali, with large hotels, a golf course of championship caliber, numerous vacation cottages and apartments, and a small strip to which air taxis fly directly from Honolulu. On this part of the island one can sit on a terrace and view the play of sun and clouds on Molokai and Lanai; through the slot between them on a good day Oahu is clearly visible.

The construction business on Maui is booming. At Wailea Beach on the southwestern side of Haleakala a massive resort development has been started which will be the equivalent in size of two Waikikis. The population of the island, now about forty thousand, will increase greatly in the coming years. The Wailea project alone when completed may eventually have fifty thousand permanent residents.

In good weather or in a four-wheel-drive vehicle one can return to Wailuku from Kaanapali by continuing around the west end of the island along a road which is in places steep, narrow, unpaved, rutty, and treacherous in wet weather. It also lacks guardrails at critical dropoffs. But on it are several picturesque Hawaiian villages in valleys with taro patches near sparkling streams, and there is an eye-filling view of the rugged coast. Taro, an important food of most Pacific islanders, is a plant with broad, heart-shaped leaves and a large, starchy root, both of which are cooked and eaten. In some islands the root is merely boiled or baked; the Hawaiians pound the boiled root with water into a paste called *poi*, typically eaten by swirling the fingers in the poi bowl and then popping the fingers into the mouth. Depending on its thickness the paste is called "one-finger," "two-finger," or "three-finger" poi.

Visitors sometimes take a pre-dawn ride from Wailuku to the top of Haleakala. Sunrise and sunset from Haleakala are both unforgettable, but there is a better chance of seeing a sunrise, for often clouds drift into the crater and across the lower mountain later in the day, obscuring the view. Headlights reveal cane fields on either side of the road at the start of the thirty-eight mile drive upward; farther on are grazing lands with occasional groves of eucalyptus.

The road enters Haleakala National Park at 6,740 feet above sea level, still more than ten miles from the summit. The air is chill and continues to grow colder on the climb. At the top snow may fall several times a year, but it does not stay long. The major Haleakala lookout, at an elevation of just under ten thousand feet, has an enclosed building in which to escape the wind. On the walls of the room are various maps, photographs, and informative diagrams of the mountain; other displays are in small cases. Large windows look into a black void, but to the east the sky is beginning to grow light.

Haleakala is actually younger than the West Maui Mountains. It last erupted from its flank little more than two centuries ago —a mere instant in geological time—and so is classed as "dormant," rather than "extinct." Its name, "The House of the Sun," derives from a Hawaiian legend concerning the famous Polynesian god Maui (his name is spelled the same as that of the island but is properly pronounced a little differently: Māui). In former days, the legend states, the sun moved so rapidly that Maui's mother, Hina, had difficulty drying her *tapa* (bark cloth). Maui climbed to the top of Haleakala, where the morning sun was accustomed to climb over the edge of the mountain, and succeeded in trapping one of its legs in a snare. After a battle, the sun agreed to move more slowly across the sky during the summer months, as it does to this day. Maui is also reported to have performed other useful feats, including raising the sky (once too low), discovering fire, and pulling the islands of Polynesia from the ocean depths with his magic fishhook.

As the sky brightens, the gulf below slowly takes shape, and it is possible to make out features along its walls and in its bottom. The sun finally appears, flooding the crater with light. "The largest inactive volcanic crater on earth," it is not a neat round crater like Diamond Head, but a huge irregular hole two miles wide and seven miles long, as big as Manhattan from the Battery to the far end of Central Park. Actually, scientists tell us that although the mountain was volcanic, this huge depression is largely the result of erosion. From the floor several thousand feet below rise cinder cones of various colors, the result of later volcanic activity, their height—actually hundreds of feet— dwarfed by the immensity of the crater. The west end of the crater is a desert, but at the east end a forest flourishes. A large gap runs south through the rim down to the ocean. The Park Service maintains several cabins for hikers within Haleakala.

The highest point on the rim of Haleakala, Red Hill, is at the road's end. At this "drive-in mountaintop" stands a group of buildings where scientists from the Universities of Hawaii and Michigan, the Smithsonian Institution, the Air Force, and the Federal Aviation Agency conduct astronomical, astrophysical, and space studies with a variety of highly sophisticated optical and electronic equipment. One of their cameras can photograph an object as small as a basketball 25,000 miles away. This is "Science City," partially deserted during the day when the scientists return to their homes at lower levels, but the scene of much activity at night. Routine tasks performed at Science City also include radar flight control and television transmission—picking up and relaying broadcasts from Oahu.

Haleakala has two other interesting sights. One, "the spectre of the Brocken," can sometimes be observed from points along the rim when the sun is low and the weather right. This phenomenon is a complete circular rainbow against a cloud with one's own shadow in the center. You may have seen something similar when flying above the clouds in an airplane: a circular rainbow with the plane's shadow at the center. Then there is the rare silversword, now rigidly protected from souvenir collectors, which grows only on Hawaii's highest mountains. The long, thin, fuzzy, silvery leaves of the young clumplike plant are in themselves unusually beautiful; after several years of growth the mature plant sends up a single vertical stalk up to six feet high bearing hundreds of bright flowers. It blooms but once.

Back at sea level, the fifty-five-mile road around the base of Haleakala to Hana, at Maui's east tip, is paved but narrow, winding in and out of the mouths of over thirty valleys and gorges cut by streams running down Haleakala's side. At several villages we see Hawaiians cultivating their staple food in centuries-old taro fields. Hana was formerly the site of a sugar plantation, but the cane land is now devoted to ranching. Today the scenic beauty and quiet of the surrounding region attract vacationers to a deluxe one-story hotel which fits gracefully into the little town. Hana still has much of the flavor of an older Hawaii, including the Hasegawa General Store, the subject of a lilting song.

The rare silversword plant grows on the nearly barren ten-thousand-foot summit of Haleakala.

About ten miles beyond Hana, Kipahulu Valley meets the sea, with the Seven Sacred Pools, a series of waterfall-linked pools carved by the rushing stream in the lava rock, at its lower end. Back from the small river, cattle graze. Farther up the valley, waterfalls and pools continue, and the valley extends through an unspoiled tropical rain forest, the home of rare plants and birds. An intensive drive to preserve this region forever was successful when a campaign headed by prominent citizens of Hawaii and supported by such well-known friends of nature as Laurance Rockefeller, Charles Lindbergh, and Arthur Godfrey succeeded in raising $600,000 and gifts of valley land. Early in 1969 it was announced that 4,235 acres, extending from the National Park at the top of Haleakala to the mouth of Kipahulu River, had been transferred to the United States Park Service. The general public will be allowed in the lower part of the valley; the upper part may be visited only by scientists.

HAWAII,
THE BIG ISLAND

According to one Hawaiian legend the volcanoes on the various islands were created by Pele, the volcano goddess, as she fled from battle (with another goddess, over a man). She went first to Kauai (Puu ka Pele—Pele's Hill—can be seen on the rim of Waimea Canyon), then to Oahu, to Molokai, to Maui, and finally to the island of Hawaii, where she established her permanent home. Interestingly, this description parallels some scientists' theories concerning the progress of volcanism in the Hawaiian chain: the islands to the northwest are older, those to the southeast younger.* Pele must also have become more skillful at island-building as she went along, for Oahu is larger than Kauai, and Maui larger than Oahu. Hawaii, where she presumably now resides, is the biggest, and it is still growing.

Because a natural confusion can arise between Hawaii as the name of the entire state and Hawaii as the name of the largest island within the state, let us use the nickname "The Big Island" when referring to the southernmost Hawaiian island. Big it is:

---

*Some recent investigators suggest that the islands arose one after another at the same spot and then drifted northwest as the ocean floor moved.

over four thousand square miles (bigger than Delaware and Rhode Island put together), taller by more than half a mile than Maui, with bigger forests and trees and producing more sugar, beef cattle, lumber, orchids, anthuriums, macadamia nuts, and coffee than any other island in the state.

Roughly triangular, the Big Island is the result of volcanic activity in five major locations. One volcano, long extinct and eroded into ridges and valleys, formed the Kohala Mountains at the island's north end. Farther south, as the island widens out, are two dormant volcanoes, Hualalai on the west (8,721 feet high), which last erupted in 1801, and Hawaii's tallest, Mauna Kea (13,796 feet) to the east. To the south are Hawaii's still-active volcanoes, Mauna Loa and Kilauea. Mauna Loa ("Long Mountain") is a little more than a hundred feet shorter than Mauna Kea ("White Mountain"), but is much more massive. Kilauea is the baby of the island, not quite 4,000 feet tall. Indeed, without knowing the scientific evidence one might suppose it to be nothing more than a side door into Mauna Loa, but its internal plumbing apparently belongs to a different system; perhaps over hundreds of thousands of years it may build to the height of Mauna Loa or Mauna Kea. At the tops of both Mauna Loa and Kilauea are depressed craters of the type a volcanologist calls a "caldera," where eruptions may occur. They also have down their sides several rift zones, lines of weakness along which the volcano may crack open and allow lava to pour forth until the pressure is relieved.

Flying from Kahului to Hilo, one sees Upolu Point at the north of the Kohala Mountains, with the town of Hawi (pronounced Hah-vee—in some words the Hawaiian *w* has a *v* sound) and the fields of the Kohala Sugar Company behind it. Along the steep northeast coast several large deep valleys reach back into the mountains. Particularly dramatic with its cliff-bordered beach is historic Waipio Valley, accessible from the land by foot, mule, or jeep. Once the home of tens of thousands of Hawaiians, the valley today has only a few families, mostly engaged in taro growing. In recent years the Peace Corps has had a training site in the valley. Between here and Hilo along the

Hamakua Coast, fifty miles of cliffs several hundred feet high were formed by the action of the ocean on the flank of Mauna Kea, which raises its irregular top in the background. Back from the cliffs, through miles of sugar cane, a road runs past the towns of the Hamakua Coast plantations. Enough rain falls so that irrigation is not necessary, and from some fields cane is transported to the mill by flume, rather than by truck.

Hilo, the second largest city in the state, with a population of over 26,000, lies around a crescent-shaped bay with a large breakwater protecting its piers from the Pacific swells. Hilo has a good deal of small-town charm, though large hotels rising on the peninsula to the south of the city center indicate that growth may soon transform it. The Hilo airport, a few years ago used only by interisland planes, is now one of Hawaii's two gateways, with jets arriving and departing on direct flights from the mainland.

The underwater configuration of Hilo Bay tends to cause tidal waves to build up to unusual heights, and twice in recent years Hilo has suffered heavy destruction. As a result, the low waterfront of the bay, where houses and businesses were destroyed, has been cleared and now contains a park and a waterfront highway. Another menace to Hilo, from the other direction, is the northeast rift of Mauna Loa. Several times in recorded history lava bursting from this zone has rushed toward Hilo, extending fingers of fire that threatened to engulf the city and fill up the Big Island's best natural harbor. A 1941 flow poured to within twelve miles of the city; in 1881 lava rolled within the present outskirts of Hilo. A huge earth and rock dam which might divert future flows has been proposed, but no action has been taken. Hilo's heavy rainfall provides an ideal climate for the commercial growing of orchids and anthuriums, which are flown in large quantities to Honolulu and the mainland.

In the front yard of the Hilo County Library lies a large block of basalt called the Naha Stone. According to tradition, this rock was used to test claimants to the position of high chief. Before going on to become king of the islands, Kamehameha lifted it (some say he merely turned it over). It must easily weigh a ton;

no single person is reported to have budged it since. Hilo's museum, the Lyman House, built of hand-hewn timbers and boards by a missionary educator in 1839, contains an amazingly varied collection of missionary materials, old Hawaiian artifacts, rare books and pictures, and scientific displays. A fireproof museum is planned to house this irreplaceable collection, and the house will then be refurnished as it was in the early days.

Kilauea volcano is a fast thirty-mile drive along a road which leads steadily uphill from Hilo. After several miles of cane fields one passes a road leading off to one of the Big Island's several macadamia nut plantations. The macadamia was introduced to Hawaii from Australia, where it is called the Queensland nut. A macadamia orchard is always attractive, since the trees do not shed their hollylike leaves seasonally. The round, marble-sized nut is encased in an extremely tough shell, which an ordinary nutcracker won't dent. Cracked by special machinery, roasted, and vacuum-packed in cans and bottles, the nuts bring premium prices. Macadamia production has increased greatly since 1960 but still cannot keep up with the growing demand.

At higher levels the road to Kilauea passes through rain forest. Particularly noticeable are tree ferns of several types, some of which may reach a height of nearly forty feet. In the middle of the last century *pulu,* the soft, silky fibers covering the young fronds of the tree fern (used for stuffing pillows and mattresses) was an important item of commerce. Today the fibrous trunks are in demand as logs for "Hawaiian sculpture" and as a growing medium for orchids and anthuriums; the Park's ferns must be constantly guarded against "tree-fern raiders."

Hawaii Volcanoes National Park, maintained by the Department of the Interior, includes the caldera area of Kilauea and fans out in one direction to take in a stretch of the south coast, a dozen miles away. In another direction the park land extends in a band up the side of Mauna Loa to include its summit caldera. From the Volcano House, a park hotel perched on the very rim of the Kilauea caldera ("Kilauea Crater"), visitors get their first view of the great hole caused thousands of years ago when the draining off of lava caused the summit of the volcano to collapse. Surrounded by cliffs on all but its southern side, its relatively flat floor lies nearly five hundred feet below, an oval roughly two and a half miles long and two miles wide. Near the lookout, at the top of the cliff, clouds of steam come from an underground hot area. At various spots on Kilauea's floor other steam vents are active. On the rim at the west side of the caldera stand the buildings of the Volcano Observatory, center of volcanological research. The main attraction, near the far side of Kilauea's floor, is the firepit of Halemaumau, a deeper hole about half a mile in diameter. From it rise clouds of smoke. Pele is putting on a show!

Neither Mauna Loa nor Kilauea is continuously active; months or years may pass without an eruption. Mauna Loa has averaged an eruption every three and a half years. Throughout most of the nineteenth century and the first quarter of this century Kilauea's activity was nearly continuous, with Halemaumau a fiery lake that sometimes overflowed onto the larger floor of the caldera. In 1924 the lava lake in Halemaumau drained away rapidly, and a series of steam blast explosions occurred, probably caused by ground water entering extremely hot areas. At the end of this activity, Halemaumau had doubled its diameter to its present size, and its floor had dropped 1,500 feet below its rim. During the next ten years, seven small eruptions reduced the depth of the Halemaumau firepit by half, and then Kilauea was inactive for nearly twenty years. In 1951, however, a new cycle of volcanic activity began, and a number of eruptions in the firepit, on the floor of Kilauea caldera, and at various places along the rift zone to the southeast have followed. An eruption which began in late 1967 and lasted over halfway through 1968 was the longest continuous activity in Halemaumau since 1924. Rift zone eruptions since 1968 have been numerous, spectacular, and extensive, wiping out stretches of a National Park road and on several occasions sending six-mile-long lava flows south to the sea.

The easy way to get to Halemaumau is to drive there by a road that encircles Kilauea Crater, but to get a good idea of volcanism one should walk there on one of the trails established by the

Park Service. The Halemaumau Trail, called "the world's weirdest walk," descends through a thick forest along broken-down ledges and ancient cracks in the earth; the forest thins out and finally ends. Cairns and metal markers lead across the old lava of the caldera floor to the brink of Halemaumau. This is a "self-guiding trail"; at the start hikers pick up a pamphlet keyed to numbered stakes along the trail which identify trees, plants, and geological features.

Lava flows come in two forms: the smooth or ropy-surfaced *pahoehoe*, which often looks like the results of a gigantic taffy-pull, and the rough, clinkery-surfaced *aa*. *Aa* and *pahoehoe* are alike chemically; their physical difference is believed caused by differences in viscosity and dissolved gases as the lava flows and cools. When erupting lava shoots high in the air, the liquid gobs may partly solidify before reaching the ground, building a cinder cone or a spatter cone.

The caldera floor is *pahoehoe*. (*Aa* is extremely abrasive and can reduce a pair of soles to shreds in a few miles.) Although the crater floor is mostly barren, in some of the cracks *ohelo* berries, edible but formerly considered sacred to Pele, grow on bushes a foot or two high. Near Halemaumau the trail takes a detour around a roped-off portion of the rim; large cracks indicate that it may be in danger of tumbling into the firepit. The safe portion of the rim, where visitors are allowed, is at the southeast side. A large parking lot there is filled with cars and tour buses whose passengers have come for a view of Hawaii's drive-in volcano. In general, people run toward—not away from—Hawaiian eruptions in order to see the spectacle; at times traffic becomes a problem.

Halemaumau's action, only a few hundred feet below, includes several pulsing fountains which have produced spatter cones sixty to eighty feet high. From time to time pieces break off a cone and tumble into the surrounding lake, which boils and surges in active regions; farther away there is a scum of partially hardened lava over the surface, and near the walls of the pit a raised rim of hardened lava has formed. A whooshing sound accompanies the activity. The fountains of lava are spectacular,

Kilauea Iki's 1959 eruption was the most spectacular ever seen on the Big Island.

but perhaps the most unusual sight is the sloshing and beating of the liquid lava upon the sides of the cones and portions of the rim. It behaves exactly like waves on a shore. Sulfurous smoke from the pit is borne intermittently toward the lookout, causing eyes to water; some people cover their noses with handkerchiefs.

By night one loses a good deal of the general perspective of the eruption, but the brilliance of the fire is tremendously increased. Ejected fragments of lava which by daylight would have been gray or black blobs now glow brightly, and the cracks on the surface of the lake—in the daytime a dull orange—form a bright, slowly changing, lacy pattern.

Kilauea Iki (Little Kilauea), a formerly deep crater just to the east of the main Kilauea caldera and separated from it by a high, relatively narrow barrier, was the scene of Kilauea's most amazing eruption in 1959. Lava burst forth from its side under great pressure and spurted to astounding heights, up to 1,900 feet (over a third of a mile) in the air! This eruption put over four hundred feet of new lava into Kilauea Iki; its cinders and spatter created a large new hill over a hundred feet high and buried nearly half a mile of park road.

The whole southeastern part of the island of Hawaii has been built by eruptions from Mauna Loa and from the eastern rift zone of Kilauea. Along this rift lies the "Chain of Craters." These nine pit craters are part of Kilauea's system; several of them have erupted since 1960 and indeed one was buried under lava in 1969. Kapoho, a little farming village nearly thirty miles from Kilauea's caldera, was destroyed in 1960 by a flank eruption which began right in the village's "back yard" and pushed out to the sea. About four-fifths of a square mile of new land was added to the Big Island's area where the lava entered the sea.

Under certain conditions, when hot lava meets the cold sea water, small, glassy fragments are formed which may accumulate along the shoreline to form a black sand beach, such as the beautiful one at Kalapana, on the Big Island's south coast.

Several other volcanic phenomena in or near the National Park are worth a visit. A lava tube is a tunnel-like structure up to twenty feet in diameter formed when a stream of flowing *pahoehoe* develops a crust around its sides and top, from which the lava drains at the end of the eruption. Inside the park area one famous tube, the Thurston Lava Tube, has been equipped with lights so that visitors may walk through it.

Tree moulds are formed when lava flows through a forest of trees so large that instead of being immediately consumed they cause a thick coating of lava to harden around them. If the entire flow remains there, the tree moulds become well-like holes in the ground after the charred trunks disintegrate. On the other hand, if the molten lava drains off downhill a series of hollow pillars is left behind. A lava flow may split and flow around higher ground, leaving an "island" of older land, called a *kipuka*, which can be identified by its bearing larger vegetation in a greater variety than newer lava will support. Quite fresh lava is of course barren, but with time and disintegration becomes

Columnar tree moulds are formed when lava flows through a forest and then drains off.

fertile soil—that's how Hawaii's great agricultural lands were formed.

Volcanic eruptions cannot be accurately predicted; however, with sensitive instruments scientists are able to detect the sort of movement of the earth that indicates when the molten lava (called magma) is moving restlessly underground. Furthermore, an increase in pressure of the magma actually causes the top of a volcano to swell a measurable amount. These indicators, along with small changes in the earth's magnetism, may indicate the likelihood of an approaching eruption, but not exactly when or where it will occur.

From the National Park the road between Mauna Loa and the coast leads through the Ka'u district and then up the Kona (leeward) side of the island. Near the Park boundry a trail leads for a mile into the Ka'u Desert, which offers a good close-up view of an *aa* flow and the "lava footprints." Keoua, cousin of Kamehameha and his rival for the Big Island's kingship, was returning through this area with his army following a battle between the two forces in 1790. Kilauea suddenly produced one of its two explosive eruptions in recorded history, killing many of Keoua's warriors. Dust and ash from the explosion, turned to mud by a rainstorm, fell over a wide area. Keoua's fleeing men left their footprints in the mud, which then hardened.

Past the Ka'u Desert are more sugar lands. The small neighboring towns of Naalehu and Waiohinu both claim to be the southernmost towns in the United States. The southernmost spot of land in any of the fifty states, South Point, visited mostly by fishermen, campers, and archeologists, is about ten miles down a side road.

In the next thirty miles the road turns north and crosses a dozen or more identifiable flows that have headed toward the sea from fissures opening in Mauna Loa's very active southwest rift. For many of them, signs have been erected giving the date of the flow; a few flows have names as well. Such eruptions may last from a few hours to a few weeks and may pour forth amazing quantities of material. The 1950 eruption alone, which covered over a mile of the highway, produced in twenty-three days an estimated 600 million cubic yards, or a billion tons, of lava. It formed six major flows, of which three reached the sea.

The Kona district of the Big Island, possessing neither a large harbor nor good sugar lands, was for years a relaxed, rather sleepy area. It had some ranches and grew a coffee of excellent flavor, with the result that the school year was adjusted so that the children could work at the coffee harvest. The sport fishing off the coast drew a few enthusiasts from distant places, but was mostly enjoyed by Kona people and a few visitors from Hilo or Honolulu. A number of Hawaiians, for whom fishing was a way of life rather than a sport, lived in small villages.

Now the Kona Coast and the Kohala Coast farther north are the scene of great tourist and residential development. Hotels already in operation include a Hilton and the Rockefeller Mauna Kea Beach Hotel; many others are built or are in the building or planning stages. Residential subdivisions have been laid out; at one site a project which may one day be a city of 20,000 is envisioned. New parks will be created and existing ones improved. The state has constructed a new airport to replace the inadequate Kona strip. The value of the coffee crop declined fifty percent in the 1960's, and the "coffee-schedule" school calendar was abandoned.

Of course, the problem facing Kona and Kohala is that which faces other parts of the state and other islands of the Pacific: how to enjoy a thriving tourist business and still preserve the individuality, the charm, and the historical sites of an area.

Kona is full of historical sites. On its hillsides lie the overgrown remains of *holua* slides, where races were held down slopes so steep that the contestants' sleds hurtled at breakneck speeds without snow. On a point projecting into the ocean at Honaunau stands the great City of Refuge, with ten-foot-high walls built of huge rocks along its landward sides. In the old days those who had committed serious violations fled to it to escape death or other punishment. The City of Refuge is now a National Historical Park, and one of the most sacred wooden temples which once stood within its walls has been authentically reconstructed.

A few miles up the coast, near the shores of Kealakekua Bay, stand the ruins of a *heiau* (stone temple); not far away is a monument to Henry Opukahaia, a young Hawaiian from this district who begged to be taken to New England for education so that he might preach Christianity to his people. An obelisk on the point across the bay was erected by the English in honor of Captain Cook, who sailed his two vessels into Kealakekua Bay in early 1779 and about a month later was killed in a brief battle between the English and the Hawaiians on the north shore of the bay. A bronze plaque marks the spot.

The town of Kailua (officially renamed Kailua-Kona to distinguish it from another Kailua on Oahu) is the heart of Kona. It was a favorite place of residence of Hawaiian royalty; Kamehameha died there in 1819. Hulihe'e Palace was built in 1837 by John Adams Kuakini, governor of the Big Island, and was later used as a summer palace by King Kalakaua. Today it is a museum containing furniture of the Kalakaua period and many historic items.

Across the street is Mokuaikaua Church, marking one of Hawaii's most important religious sites. When the brig *Thaddeus* brought the missionaries from New England in 1820, Kailua was their first port of call. They met the king and explained their purpose; part of the missionary company stayed and operated a mission for six months while the others went on to Honolulu and Kauai. Although the Kailua missionaries then moved to Honolulu themselves, they returned after three years to find that governor Kuakini had built a small church, the first Mokuaikaua. So rapidly did the new religion spread that in 1826 a new larger church was constructed.

The present stone-walled building was erected in 1835, after someone with a grudge against the second church had burned it down, and dedicated in 1837. The timbers used in the building are hand-hewn from native trees and joined with wooden pins rather than nails. Somewhat smaller than the building it replaced, it is a jewel of a church, and other churches in the islands derived their architecture from it. Its spire, which once dominated the little town, has received competition from high-rise hotels. A four-story height limit for construction in Kailua, belatedly approved by the Big Island Board of Supervisors, did not affect buildings already completed or planned.

The Big Island leads the state in the production of beef. The first cattle were brought to Hawaii from California in the 1790's on two visits by the British explorer Captain George Vancouver. Released on a plateau in the north central part of the Big Island, they throve and multiplied, protected by a ten-year *kapu (tabu)* at King Kamehameha's orders. Ranches of domesticated cattle were later established, and in 1846 there were over 25,000 wild cattle and 10,000 tame cattle on the various islands. Beginning about 1830 the hides, tallow, and later the salted beef from these animals became important in the Hawaiian economy. Spanish or Mexican cowboys were brought in to help operate the ranches; although their skills were soon acquired by Hawaiians, today the Hawaiian word for cowboy is still *paniolo* (Spaniard).

To the Big Island cattle region about 1815 came a sailor, John Palmer Parker, who was first a hunter of wild cattle and later a rancher. The Parker Ranch, still run by one of his descendants, is the largest in the state. Indeed, its more than a quarter million acres of land made it for years the largest singly-owned ranch under the American flag.

Although beef ranks first among agricultural products produced for purely local consumption, Hawaii's ranches raise only about half of the beef consumed in the state. The rest is imported from the Mainland and from Australia and New Zealand.

One of the Big Island's ranchers, Herbert Shipman, performed a noteworthy public service by preserving the rare *nene* goose, Hawaii's state bird, from extinction. It had nearly been wiped out by hunters, cats, dogs, and mongooses. From a total of perhaps twenty-five birds, the population has been slowly built up to several hundred. Young birds hatched in captivity are released in sanctuaries on both the Big Island and Maui. By the way, the mongoose, a rodent originally from India, was brought to Hawaii in 1883 from Jamaica in an attempt to reduce the rat population of the cane fields. Unfortunately the mongoose displayed toward the rats a typically Hawaiian spirit of tolerance, so that Hawaii now has *both* rats and mongooses.

The road north from Kona leads through Parker Ranch lands at elevations of one to three thousand feet. Except for the Pacific, often visible some miles away, we might be in cow country in one of our western states. There's even a kind of prickly pear cactus growing here and there. Waimea (or Kamuela), the Parker Ranch center, looks a good deal like a western town, and recent building has tried to maintain that appearance.

About ten miles downhill from Waimea is the port of Kawaihae, where cattle are loaded for the trip to Oahu. Not far from the port are two large *heiau*s on either side of a road. The upper one, which dominates a hilltop, is in quite good condition. From it one gets a fine view of the coast southward and of Mount Hualalai, rising behind North Kona. A plaque tells us that Kamehameha built this *heiau* in 1791–1792 after a prophet had said that if he built such a *heiau* in honor of his war god Kukailimoku he would become supreme ruler of the Big Island. In the summer of 1791 the body of Kamehameha's slain rival, Keoua, was offered as a sacrifice on the altar, fulfilling the prophecy.

In another direction from Waimea lies the snow-dotted top of Mauna Kea, less than twenty miles distant. Hawaii's summits are valuable sites for scientific work, and 13,796-foot-high Mauna Kea is the most highly prized. Mauna Kea's installations include a new observatory with the best viewing platform in the northern hemisphere and facilities for atmospheric study. The observatory has two twenty-four-inch telescopes and an eighty-eight-inch telescope whose two-and-a-half-ton mirror cost three million dollars. In 1971 astronomers using this equipment reported several major discoveries concerning the planet Jupiter.

Mauna Kea has a few other interesting features. One of the cones at the top contains a small lake, whose sediments are being studied by scientists. Not far from the top is a quarry, to which in olden times the Hawaiians came for a particularly hard stone used in making tools and weapons. For several months out of the year skiing is possible on Mauna Kea, although the few hardy skiers face a bumpy jeep ride and a lung-straining hike in the thin air before getting to the slopes. A new access road, planned for the future, may make tropical skiing more popular. Thousands of years ago, according to scientific evidence, year-round skiing would have been possible—the top of the mountain was covered by a 250-foot-thick glacier during the Ice Age.

THE PACIFIC VIEW

The Pacific islands, which in 1800 were about ninety-nine percent populated by native peoples, today show a great diversity of societies, governments, and economies. Everywhere the interaction between Western civilization and indigenous cultures which were entirely differently oriented is to be seen. There are regions where the indigenous culture has been almost completely obliterated, places where it has blended with the foreign culture, and places where it still predominates. On many islands, every child goes to school and learns to read and write a European language; yet in a place such as New Guinea many elected legislators are unable to read and write any language. In some regions subsistence agriculture is still the primary way of life, and most demands are filled by materials at hand. Yet once the objects of Western civilization—from axes to airplanes—are introduced, the people do not reject them but try to find some way to afford them.

The nineteenth century saw great changes introduced to the Pacific by ships from outside. Whaling became the ocean's biggest business and then died. Traders, missionaries, and planters came and remained, followed by the big nineteenth-century wave of colonialism. Worldwide, the twentieth century has been one of accelerated change. In the Pacific new methods of transportation and communication have had striking effects. Whereas only a few generations ago a canoe manned by hardy Marshallese sailors might have sailed and paddled from Majuro to Kwajalein in from three days to a week, navigating by stick charts, today entire families can make the trip in forty minutes. Other Pacific changes have been equally striking.

But there are many Pacific oceans—or many ways of looking at the Pacific—depending on one's position and interests. Dr. Force of the Bishop Museum had offered an anthropologist's view. Other men have their own Pacific oceans and it may be of significance to learn what some of these men think about the Pacific today and tomorrow.

At Camp Holland M. Smith, on a hill overlooking Pearl Harbor, is the headquarters of the Commander-in-Chief of the Pacific (CINCPAC), who is in charge of American ships, planes, and the many men stationed in Asia (Korea, Vietnam, and Thailand), the Philippines, Japan, Okinawa, Guam, and Hawaii—to name the most important—and spread over about 85 million square miles (over two-fifths) of the surface of the globe. The military protection of the Pacific, America's western frontier, while involving all of America's armed forces, seems logically to be the prime responsibility of the U. S. Navy. In April 1968 the key position of CINCPAC passed to Admiral John S. McCain, Jr.

In defending the Pacific, the military faces the problems of great distance, the possible abandonment or cutting back of some of our western bases, and advances in technology of warfare and is concerned indirectly but vitally with America's diplomatic and economic relations with Pacific countries. Russia, Red China, North Vietnam, and North Korea are all Pacific nations. Of the area which his command covers, Admiral McCain said: "There are twenty different flags in addition to our own flown in this vast segment of our planet. Of these, nine can be considered firm, consistent friends of our country. The alignments of the remainder are either definitely hostile to our interests or vary between latent hostility and nonalignment."

Besides Korea, the China coast, and Vietnam, Admiral

McCain listed "no less than eight other Pacific command areas which must be classed as actual or potential trouble spots. These are Laos, Cambodia, Indonesia, the Philippines, Thailand, Malaysia, Singapore, and the Taiwan Strait." At present, America's strongest allies in the area include Japan, South Korea, Taiwan, Thailand, and of course Australia and New Zealand. South Vietnam may remain an ally.

With the British withdrawal from a strong position at Singapore, Admiral McCain sees the Indian Ocean as an important area in which America should establish a base. Russia has already sent a squadron into the Indian Ocean, and threatens to be ready to fill the vacuum left by the British withdrawal. According to the Admiral: "We have to be on our guard all over the world." He also is firm in pointing out that the most important of the major decisions involving the military are not made by the military, but are executed by the armed forces "as ordered by the President of the United States. There may be considerable dialogue among the military on what course of action is necessary to do the job. But one of the fine things about this United States is this civilian authority."

Pacific affairs involve much more than armed forces and military bases; they concern the general welfare of Pacific peoples. A caution against continuing the past reliance on military might, treaties, and foreign aid in shaping the future of the Pacific was made by Dr. David E. Lilienthal in a speech in Tokyo in 1968. He believes that "policies of mutual trade" are the best nonviolent way of "influencing events and developing the best that is in people." He said further that "the twenty-first century does not belong to the Atlantic, but to the Pacific" and that he hoped the "strong desire among some Americans to withdraw from the life and future of the Pacific Basin"—as a result of the Vietnam experience—will not "lead the United States to insulate itself from responsibilities in the Pacific Ocean."

One person who feels very strongly that Hawaii is the key to American participation in Pacific affairs is John A. Burns, Governor of the State of Hawaii. "How can Hawaii lead in Pacific affairs?" he was asked.

"Hawaii already *is* a leader in the Pacific in many ways," said Governor Burns. "In its advanced political and social climate, its racial and religious harmony among persons of diverse ancestries and philosophies, it leads by example. It shows to other Pacific lands how general prosperity and advancement can be generated in a community firmly based on a foundation of American political principles—freedom of speech and press, free elections, freedom of movement and of business enterprise.

"Hawaii has proven that prosperity and a reasonable degree of happiness are the fruits of a well-ordered society in which human dignity, and all that contributes to human dignity, have the highest priority. Hawaii's citizens unite freely in a variety of organizations—in community associations, in labor unions, in management associations, in business cooperatives, in religious, social, and fraternal societies—to share their ideas, talents, and special skills in improving our society. Hawaii's community offers light and encouragement to millions simply by being where it is and what it is."

At the University of Hawaii, Dr. George P. Woollard, Director of the Hawaii Institute of Geophysics, was solicited for a scientist's view of the Pacific. The air, land, water, and what lies under the water all come under one or more of the major branches of the institute's studies—physical oceanography, geochemistry, solid-earth geophysics, meteorology and cloud physics, geology, and soils and sediments. What do geoscientists find especially interesting about the Pacific?

"The fact that we know so little about it, for one thing," Dr. Woollard replied, going on to point out how much more geophysical work, relatively, had been done in Atlantic areas. Our concept of the earth and its crust has changed greatly in recent years, Dr. Woollard explained. The surface of the earth was formerly considered static, but now scientists know that it's dynamic. Spreading seems to be taking place from cracks or ridges in the ocean floors. In the Atlantic, where the spreading is taking place from the Mid-Atlantic Ridge, the continents—the Americas to the west and Europe and Africa to the east—are drifting apart and rotating along with the movements of the ocean's bed.

(One can see that the two sets of continents would once have fit together.) The spreading in the Pacific Basin seems to be operating differently. Here the continents act as buttresses, and the spreading crust in the ocean bed is "diving underneath" the continental masses and pushing them upward. "This would account for the ring of trenches around the Pacific, the island arcs, the volcanoes, and the seismic activity of a sort which you get nowhere else in the world," said Dr. Woollard.

At present the Pacific areas being intensively studied are the fracture zones extending across the Pacific bed, the boundary areas between the ocean and the land, and some of the affected land masses. Many interrelationships between the ocean, the atmosphere, the ionosphere, seismic activity, and sunspots need to be further explored.

Dr. Woollard explained that the Hawaii Institute of Geophysics is now concentrating on gathering fundamental knowledge. Eventually will come the applications of that knowledge, and perhaps in the future, practical benefits may be the "selling point" for continuing research. Weather forecasting and tidal-wave research are of obvious practical value. But Dr. Woollard feels that the most important practical applications of Pacific scientific research will be determined by two needs: national defense and the expanding world population's demand for food. If another major war should come—and there is nothing in the history of man to guarantee that it might not—accurate and extensive knowledge of the Pacific Ocean will be crucial. The food problem too is international rather than national. Protein is needed. We need to know what controls the migrations of fish, to find better ways of catching them, to see if fish can be herded, and to manage the ocean's marine life properly. More interdisciplinary work in oceanic ecology must be conducted by geoscientists and biological scientists.

Dr. Woollard mentioned briefly an economic phenomenon of possibly drastic consequence to the Pacific which first drew public attention in early 1969—the population explosion of the "Crown of Thorns" starfish. This sixteen-armed starfish was considered a great rarity until a few years ago, and those that were found were usually small. Now they have appeared in great numbers, in sizes ranging up to two feet across, in many parts of the Pacific—the Great Barrier Reef off Australia, the islands of Micronesia, and elsewhere.

The large, razor-sharp spines which cover the Crown of Thorns contain a poison. Even worse is the fact that it eats live coral in large quantities, perhaps a dozen square feet per month. Within two years after one was first casually noticed in the waters off Guam, an army of these starfish had moved along the reef, devouring as they went, and, according to one scientist, "a twenty-four mile stretch of the reef along Guam's northern coast has been eaten away, leaving nothing but dead coral skeletons. It will be years before the living coral organisms will be able to build back the coral."

Dead coral cannot withstand wave action. Without a protective reef, low islands would rapidly disappear, and the higher islands would suffer increased erosion. In the absence of coral, many food fish would die out because they would have lost their habitat or their own source of food. Furthermore, it is feared that on the dead coral a sort of algae will grow which will cause normally wholesome food fish to become violently poisonous.

Like other starfish, the Crown of Thorns cannot be killed by cutting it in pieces; a starfish cut in half grows into two starfish. Injection of each animal with a chemical will kill it, but that is a slow process. During the summer of 1969, about ten teams of marine scientists, including some from the University of Hawaii, went to Micronesia to study the starfish threat, hoping to explain how it came about and to devise ways of coping with it. Preliminary reports indicate that the problem is even more serious than had been feared. Toward the end of the summer, the starfish menace was discovered in Hawaiian waters as well. Unless man or nature can stop this alarming infestation, a number of Pacific islanders will be eaten out of their homes.

Another Hawaii organization which deals with the sea is the Makapuu Oceanic Center, a scientific three-ring circus founded by a dynamic and imaginative young marine biologist, Taylor A. ("Tap") Pryor. The first of his projects was Sea Life Park, a large public exhibit which features performing porpoises and whales, sea birds, and a spectacular exhibit of coral-reef life—a huge tank where marine creatures ranging from tiny fish to hammerhead sharks are visible through windows along a spiral walkway.

The second branch of the Center, partly supported by funds from the Park, is Oceanic Institute, a nonprofit organization that conducts research of a rather practical nature which will have, as one staff member put it, "maximum impact upon ocean-related human problems." One of its important activities is investigating food from the sea through aquaculture—developing techniques which will lead to the raising of stable supplies of such fish as mullet in "fish farms" or ponds. Studies of porpoises and whales, marine ecology, marine conservation, and water pollution are also receiving attention.

Among the most interesting programs of the Institute are those in ocean engineering, which have recently included work on models of a stable ocean platform and a futuristic floating city.

The third major enterprise of the Makapuu Oceanic Center is the Makai Undersea Test Range, a commercial company which

A "Crown of Thorns" starfish eats its way across the coral reef, leaving behind a dead, barren waste.

will test underwater equipment and techniques and provide consultation and services for underwater problems of government, industrial, and academic organizations. The Makai Range has built and tested a large, mobile undersea habitat of new design, capable of holding six men for twenty days at a depth of six hundred feet. Thus men are able to live and work at the bottom of the ocean for extended periods without needing to come to the surface. As it rests on the ocean floor, the habitat is pressurized so that divers can open hatches in the bottom and go out into the surrounding water.

Taylor Pryor served by appointment of former President Johnson on a fifteen-man national Commission on Marine Sciences, which recommended the creation of a National Oceanographic and Atmospheric Agency to formulate and direct national policy involving both government and private enterprise in oceanic development. In this the Pacific Ocean would of course be important, and Hawaii might well become "the Cape Kennedy of oceanics," Pryor has said.

Drawing of sea floor habitat, Makai Range, Makapuu Oceanic Center, is as eerily elegant as a spaceship.

For a final view of the Pacific region, one turns naturally enough to Dr. Y. Baron Goto, Vice-Chancellor Emeritus of the East-West Center, a Honolulu institute supported by federal government funds. Dr. Goto was formerly head of East-West Center's Institute for Technical Interchange. Retired in 1969, he has continued working harder than ever, as a special consultant to the Center on food and agricultural programs. He is a man with a unique and intimate knowledge of Pacific peoples and problems. Over the years, his broad, genial face has turned up in coffee plantations in New Guinea, in coconut groves in the Trust Territory, and over *kava* bowls in Samoa. He has been appointed a U.S. representative to the South Pacific Commission.

In deliberate, soft-spoken tones, Dr. Goto said that he accepted the East-West Center position because he wanted to work with our Pacific neighbors—first of all those under the American flag, but others as well. He felt that in providing foreign aid the United States has not done enough for Pacific peoples.

"What is the role of the East-West Center in the Pacific?"

Dr. Goto answered: "To provide educational opportunities for the development of the people at all levels—even as far down as the coconut-root level—and more particularly to help the people of the Pacific islands better appreciate and understand each other's cultures and beliefs."

Of the nearly one thousand Pacific Islanders who came to the East-West Center in its first nine years, all but about ninety enrolled in the Institute for Technical Interchange, in programs that lasted for an average of six months, although some of them lasted only a few weeks. Other training sessions and conferences involving many more people were conducted at various places in the field. The Pacific islands represented included Australia, the Solomons, Cook Islands, Fiji, Gilbert-Ellice Islands, Guam, Nauru, New Caledonia, New Guinea, New Hebrides, New Zealand, Niue, American Samoa, Western Samoa, Tahiti, Tonga, the Trust Territory, and Wallis-Futuna. Nearly half of the people trained were from the Trust Territory.

When asked which programs had been the largest or most important, Dr. Goto mentioned tourism and travel-management programs and the development of various careers for women in such fields as nursing, office work, waitress supervision, and beauty-parlor operation. Most of the women come from cultures where traditionally women have never done any sort of work outside the family. Those who have received training will go back and teach their new skills and techniques to their own people.

East-West Center students who want academic courses take them at the University of Hawaii. However, the Institute for Technical Interchange programs do not require specific educational backgrounds on the part of the people enrolled. The aim is to train the people to apply skills and knowledge in everyday occupations. Dr. Goto also noted that at the East-West Center

On the lawn of the East-West Center, a federally supported institution on the University of Hawaii campus, cultural interchange is both an aim and an accomplishment.

the participants have a chance—many of them for the first time —to meet, live with, and begin to understand their Pacific neighbors. They learn that each group has its unique culture, and they learn to be tolerant of other cultures at the same time they are acquiring something of the feeling of a commonwealth of Pacific peoples.

When asked about the changes he sees taking place in the Pacific, and whether the tendency was to move all of the people toward a sort of common denominator, Dr. Goto said: "Changes are taking place, but in the foreseeable future I cannot see such a result. I believe it is important that each group maintain its own culture and its own practices and beliefs, to the extent that this will not limit the group's progress. A sense of self-confidence, of pride in one's own culture, is essential. In the earlier centuries, colonial powers tended to make indigenous peoples feel that their cultures were in all respects inferior. This was bad. However, one thing that I hope will take place is that eventually all of the people of the Pacific will have one common language for communication, be it English or French. This would serve to unify all of the forces in the area for the good of all."

Somewhat surprisingly, since agriculture has always been his main interest, Dr. Goto does not believe that agriculture holds much hope for the economic development of the Pacific islands. Like some of the oceanographers, he feels that the ocean itself will eventually provide the key to the economy of the area. In the meantime, tourism has given, and will continue to give, an economic boost to many places.

Dr. Goto feels that really *places* aren't developed, *people* are: that the sort of material aid which provides only roads, buildings, machines, and piers, has to be repeated decade after decade. But if people are educated to help themselves and then are given guidance, a solid foundation for future development will exist. The final question Dr. Goto was confronted with was: "What area of human activity do you think is most important in the Pacific's future?"

"Education," he said without hesitation. "For education is the key."

INDEX